The Sound of His Voice

*Discovering the Secrets
of God's Guidance*

Edward William Fudge

Edward Fudge
Prov. 3:5-6

New
Leaf
Books

ORANGE, CALIFORNIA

THE SOUND OF HIS VOICE
published by New Leaf Books

Originally published as *Beyond the Sacred Page:
A testimony to the guidance of God in the life of one man.*

Newly revised and enlarged.

COPYRIGHT 1995, 2002 by Edward William Fudge

ISBN 0-9714289-4-8
Printed in the United States of America

For information, write or call New Leaf Books, 12542 S. Fairmont,
Orange, CA 92869; 1-877-634-6004 (toll free).

Or visit our website: www.newleafbooks.org

Visit the author's website: www.EdwardFudge.com

Dedication:

For Melanie and Michael,

Jeremy and Kristy,

and those who come after them.

One generation shall praise your works to another,
  O LORD, and shall declare your mighty acts.
Your kingdom is an everlasting kingdom,
  and your dominion endures throughout all generations.

Contents

Invitation to the Reader

Do you know that the Creator, who made you and redeemed you in Jesus Christ, also desires to guide your steps each new day that comes?

God Promises to Guide His People

This is not idle talk—or merely wishful thinking. It is God's own promise, a promise that he repeats over and again throughout both Old and New Testaments. Notice just a few examples of this divine promise:

> "I will instruct you and teach you in the way which you should go; I will counsel you with My eye upon you" (Psalm 32:8).

> "Trust in the LORD with all your heart, and do not lean on your own understanding. In all your ways acknowledge Him, and He will direct your paths" (Proverbs 3:5-6).

> "Your ears will hear a word behind you, 'This is the way, walk in it,' whenever you turn to the right or to the left" (Isaiah 30:21).

> "My sheep hear My voice; and I know them, and they follow Me" (John 10:27).

"For all who are being led by the Spirit of God, these are children of God" (Romans 8:14).

Learning to Recognize God's Voice

But how does God actually lead us, other than through the general teaching of the Bible? I have asked that question myself now for more than half a century. And, by the grace of God, I have discovered a number of very specific answers—what I call "the secrets of God's guidance."

This book describes many of the ways God guides those who ask him, exactly as I have experienced them in my own Christian walk. I am certainly not the first believer to discover these truths. Indeed, I stand in a long line with thousands, perhaps even millions, of others before me. If we look at the larger Christian picture, these are not secrets at all.

I hope that this book will encourage you to seek—and to discover—God's guidance for your own life. And, when God answers your prayer for direction, I encourage you to tell someone else about his faithfulness to you. For, however it comes, nothing on earth is sweeter than "the sound of His voice."

Chapter 1

An Inner Nudge

With a child-like heart of love,
At Thy bidding may I move,
Prompt to serve and follow Thee–
Loving Him who first loved me.
                                        –Jane E. Leeson

As a civil trial lawyer in Houston, Texas, I frequently encounter tough characters. A few years now into this beat, gruff judges no longer frighten me and frowning juries do not send an automatic chill down my spine. Even blustery attorney adversaries, those who can't complete a sentence without cursing and who willfully obstruct my efforts at every turn, normally leave me unruffled. That said, nothing had prepared me for what happened when I encountered the man I will call T. J. Thompson.

The Ex-Convict with a Receptive Heart
Although afflicted with multiple sclerosis, T. J. was used to driving a car without difficulty. One morning as he approached an intersection on his way home from some errands, the driver of an empty school bus ran a stop sign directly into his path. Suddenly T. J. had to make a life-and-death choice. He could swerve head-on into oncoming traffic. Going the other way, he

would crash into a telephone pole at 35 m.p.h. Or he could keep the wheel straight and take his chances with the empty bus. He chose the bus. The school district refused to pay for his medical treatment and T. J. came to my firm for help.

Whenever a case involved unusual facts or a client presented a special challenge, a staffer would brief me by memo before the initial client conference. Such a memo preceded T. J.'s arrival to my office that day in 1993.

"This client has M.S.," the memo said, "and moves about in a motorized cart. He spent considerable time in the penitentiary in years past and he has developed quite a 'potty' mouth." The memo noted that T. J. could be demanding or even outrageous. "Unless you take firm control of the situation from the beginning," it warned, "this client may pose a constant problem."

The time came for T. J.'s initial conference and the reception-ist paged me. Things started a bit ragged when I forgot his name en route to the reception room. "Mr. Thomas?" I inquired, looking around the half-filled room. No answer. Then I spotted the small motorized cart. Walking toward its occupant, I said it again. "Mr. Thomas?"

The man sitting there glowered. "Thompson!" he said. "It's Thompson. Are you Mr. Fudge?"

"Yes," I answered. "I'm sorry, Mr. Thompson. Let's go this way to my office—it's a more direct route."

I led him down the long, straight hallway that employees used, rather than taking the usual, more impressive, half-circle past busy offices and conference rooms bustling with activity. Inside my office, I invited him to park himself across the antique oak partner's desk that once belonged to my father. After sever-al maneuvers with his vehicle, T. J. situated his cart and settled himself in it.

"I understand this is your second accident." I said, pausing for him to answer. He did not reply directly. Instead, he launched into an embittered description of his lifelong problems, generously spiced with four-letter words and other invectives. Yet his voice, which was loud even when calm, seemed to transmit pain more than belligerence. And whenever he used profanity, he instinctively lowered his tone.

Something inside me said that this man needed to ventilate, so I decided to listen rather than interrupt. Eventually he appeared to be at a stopping point. "We could probably visit all day," I said softly, "but we had better focus now on our business or we will never get through."

For the first time, he smiled. "Yes," he said. "I need to finish and go home. I take care of my 93-year-old mother, all by myself, 24 hours a day. I cannot leave the house unless someone else comes to be with her."

My inner sense was confirmed. There was more to this man than the harsh exterior. As we continued our business, that inner conviction grew. Despite T. J.'s rough background and salty language, I sensed a heart desperately lonely and wounded in many ways. "Most of all," I thought, "he needs a personal relationship with Jesus Christ." I prayed silently that God would open a door for me to witness to him about the Lord, and determined to speak out if God cleared the way.

As T. J. and I concluded our immediate business, there came another inner sense. "You should pray for this man," it seemed to say. "Now. Out loud. And touch him to demonstrate Christ's love."

As crazy as it sounded, I believed the impulse came from God. But I also knew that God does not overpower people, or impose himself on them beyond their consent. So somewhat hesitantly I said, "I would like to ask you a personal question that has nothing to do with our legal business."

He nodded. Almost before the words were framed I heard myself ask, "Do you believe in prayer?" He paused a second. "Yes," he said, with some conviction. He seemed to anticipate what might come next.

"This is very unusual," I began. "I have never been in this exact situation before, but I feel that I am supposed to pray for you. God gives us our life and health every day," I continued, "and he loves us very much. We have all sinned and broken fellowship with God. But God loves us so much he sent his son Jesus Christ to die on the cross to forgive us. Someday he will raise the dead and restore the universe he has made to its perfect state. There will be no more suffering or disease or death then."

I paused. T. J. was still listening. "Sometimes," I continued, "because he is powerful and good, and because of what Jesus accomplished by his death and resurrection, God gives healing now as well. It is a small sign of his coming kingdom, and a tangible reminder that he loves us. If you don't mind, I think I am supposed to come around there and put my hands on you while we pray."

"I would like that very much," T. J. said, twisting his spasmatic shoulders as if to prepare for what was coming next. I walked around the desk, placed both hands lightly on his shoulders and quietly began to pray. I thanked God simply for the daily gifts of life and health, and acknowledged him as the all-powerful Creator on whom we depend for existence every moment. Then, without fanfare or special words, I asked God's healing mercy on T. J.— for his multiple sclerosis, for the injuries he sustained in the automobile collision, for all the psychological and spiritual pain he carried from whatever source. Finally, I requested that God would make himself known to this man in a special way, and eventually draw T. J. to know Jesus Christ who shows us God's love in human terms.

The prayer ended, I returned to my chair behind the desk. For a moment there was an awkward silence. Then T. J. spoke. "Thank you," the ex-convict said softly, wiping the moisture from his eyes. What he related next still leaves me speechless—and confirms more than ever that the God who knows all details and circumstances of our lives had brought T. J. and me together that day.

"There is something very strange going on here," he said, struggling for words and for the composure to express them. "When I was growing up many years ago, my mother used to pray for sick people. She put her hands on them, too." His voice broke momentarily and he cleared his throat. "When she did, people often said they felt heat from her hands go through their body. My mother prayed for me many times as a child and young man. But for some reason, I never felt the heat from my mother's hands."

I trembled in awe at what my ears were hearing, and what they were about to hear next. "When you prayed just now," T. J. continued, "I felt heat coming from your hands into my shoulders—right through my clothes. And I tell you, Mr. Fudge, your hands were cool when we met a few minutes ago."

Now I was the one lacking words. "God is real and he is in charge," I said. "We can never presume what he will do, but we can always ask him for his blessing. Sometimes he responds in an immediate and obvious way." T. J. listened respectfully. "Sometimes he gives health gradually and in smaller portions," I continued. "Whether God works quickly or slowly—and to whatever extent—we must always remember to give him the praise."

The experience with T. J. was not the first time I had felt God's silent nudge. The earliest occasion I remember was far less dramatic but equally as unexpected. It occurred long before I ever became an attorney.

"Go calling around the block..."

It was a Sunday afternoon during the summer of 1974. After my father's sudden death in 1972, my wife Sara Faye and I had moved from St. Louis, Missouri to my hometown of Athens, Alabama, to assist my mother in the family's Christian publishing business. I also preached for a small Church of Christ 18 miles out in the country. And, though I regularly proclaimed God's Word to an audience of 200 people with no nervousness whatsoever, the thought of initiating a spiritual conversation one-on-one with a stranger still petrified me.

We had just finished lunch that Sunday and settled in our favorite den chairs to read the newspaper. Suddenly I felt a curious compulsion, almost as if someone were telegraphing a silent message to my mind. "Take some gospel booklets and go door-to-door around your cul-de-sac," the inner urge seemed to dictate. I had never experienced anything like this before, and frankly did not relish the thought of calling on neighbors uninvited, some of whom I had never even met. The sense persisted, however. So, convinced that this leading came from the Lord, I gathered some gospel materials and started walking dutifully around Sandra Lane.

Nobody answered at the first house or two and I sighed in secret relief. A lady responded to the doorbell at the next house. "Hello," I said, with no prepared script. "My name is Edward Fudge and I am your neighbor at the corner. I just wanted to say 'hello' and give you this booklet. If you would ever like to talk about the Bible, I would be honored to visit with you."

"Thank you," she said. "It was nice of you to come by." I walked on. "What's this about, Lord?" I prayed silently, while walking up the sidewalk. Some residents were not home. Others appeared cool and reserved. None was impolite, but was I doing any good? Was this "call" for my neighbors or for me?

Half way around the circle, at the opposite corner from mine, I found the front door open behind a locked screened door. The interior appeared unlit and the sounds of a baseball game drifted from a television somewhere in the rear of the house. I knocked on the door and waited. Shortly, a large man wearing trousers, an undershirt and a weekend beard came from the TV room to answer my knock.

"What can I do for you?" he called out as he approached the open door. From his rumpled appearance, I guessed I had waked him from his nap.

"Hello," I said, and repeated the few sentences I had put together around the block. Suddenly he sprang wide awake. "I am so glad you came," he said. "I have a real problem and I didn't know where to find an answer." He explained that he had recently begun attending a particular church and wished to join. "The minister told me I should not be baptized until I quit smoking and became sanctified," he said, "but as I read the Bible, Jesus commands me to be baptized and I don't want to wait. What do you think?"

There are some subjects about which I know little. As a lifelong member of the Churches of Christ, however, baptism is not one of them. "I believe that we should never put off doing anything we clearly understand that God commands us to do," I confidently told him. "If you believe that Jesus wants you to be baptized, I encourage you to do that as soon as possible. God will help you quit smoking later if he wants you to do that."

"What is more," I added, "I believe that God has sent me here this afternoon to tell you this very thing," and I described the strange events which had brought me to his door.

What Do These "Nudges" Mean?

What should I make of these incidents? I am not altogether sure. Both the Old and New Testaments tell us that God directs the daily lives of his people. Indeed, the Bible provides many accounts of God wondrously bringing people together to accomplish his own saving purpose. Saul goes looking for donkeys and encounters a man, Samuel. God sends Philip down a desert road where he meets an Ethiopian nobleman at a literal standstill, struggling to understand the Scriptures. God dispatches Ananias to visit the blinded persecutor of Christians, Saul of Tarsus. He sends kosher Peter to a houseful of Gentiles.

It seems so natural and ordinary in the Bible stories. But how did God actually communicate with Samuel and Peter and Philip so many years ago? Did he speak aloud? Did he bypass their ears

and address their minds? Or did he direct them by some quiet urging—what I have called an "inner nudge"? The Bible does not
always make that clear.

At first, these divine impulses caught me by total surprise. Not
for lack of faith in God, or shortage of Bible knowledge. I was surprised that he knew me—and had decided to use me in his own
grand purpose. He was not only "out there," high and holy and
sovereign over the vast expanse of stars and space. He was also
on Sandra Lane in Athens, Alabama, and in my law office in
Houston, Texas, ready to involve himself in the daily concerns of
people I could see and talk to and touch.

I had been blessed with Christian parents and a devout up-
bringing. I had been privileged to receive 19 years of outstanding
formal Christian education. Yet nothing had prepared me to
expect God's leading in this manner. In church, we sang about
moving at God's "bidding" like a trusting child, but I was still
almost incredulous when that bidding actually began to come.

TO REFLECT OR DISCUSS

1. How do you imagine that God spoke to Saul, Philip, Ananias
   and Peter? Do you think they were surprised when he did
   speak to them?

2. What is your reaction to the stories Edward relates in this
   chapter? How do you account for that reaction?

3. Have you ever felt such an "inner nudge" and wondered if it
   came from God? Did you act on that nudge? What was the
   result?

Chapter 2

"Guide, Guard and Direct Us"

Break Thou the bread of life, dear Lord, to me,
As Thou didst break the loaves beside the sea;
Beyond the sacred page I seek Thee, Lord;
My spirit pants for Thee, O living Word!

–Mary Ann Lathbury

I was born in 1944 and enjoyed an idyllic childhood, growing up in the 50's and early 60's. Our country had whipped dictators across two oceans to win World War II, and FDR's "New Deal" had sparked fresh hope and spawned opportunities at home. While I was in second grade, the adults elected a five-star general nicknamed "Ike" to a presidency which—despite a Cold War brewing with the Soviets—insinuated we could breathe deeply, relax for a while and enjoy diversions such as golf. Life generally was simple then, especially in small Southern towns and particularly to a child like me. Everything had its appropriate place and most things seemed to fit where they belonged.

A Picture Postcard Town

Athens, Alabama was a picture postcard town in that tranquil world. Comforted by rolling Appalachian foothills to the north and east, and the majestic Tennessee River to the south, the Limestone

County seat occupied a fertile farming plain half-way between Nashville, Tennessee and Birmingham, Alabama.

The town itself radiated out from the Courthouse Square, marked by an ancient traditional building of county government embellished with Corinthian columns and topped by a spired dome. Above each entrance, engraved in ancient formal capital letters, were the words "LIMESTONE COVNTY COVRT HOVSE." Beneath the dome, four stately but thunderous clocks struck the hours to citizens in all directions. In one corner of the courthouse yard a historical marker proudly proclaimed: "The County Older than the State." Across the green, a tall mute soldier faithfully kept his silent guard. Chiseled in stone, he would always wear the Confederate gray.

Each Saturday, old men dressed in overalls and armed with pocket knives occupied shady benches around the courthouse and whiled away the time. The "Spit and Whittle Club," we called them. Most Saturdays, a procession of preachers held forth on the grassy courthouse yard—vying with one another for the strictest, most parsimonious, portrayal of God's eternal grace and kingdom. Some solicited offerings, others declined them with disdain, but a few members of the ambling audience never minded pitching in a little for the entertainment. Eventually a courthouse clerk would appear at the door to request less noise outside, at which point the proceedings gradually wound down, the listeners meandered off and the whittlers had the place to themselves again. There was not too much to do in Athens on a Saturday.

My 7,000 neighbors lived quiet and peaceable lives in so many wood, shingle or brick houses along serene streets adorned with marigolds, buttercups and chrysanthemums according to season, and canopied by maples, oaks and pines. There were less fortunate parts of town, of course, black and white respectively. I rarely had occasion to go there, and it did not occur to me that some townspeople might have visions of life different from my own. Nor did I think for a minute of the wicked prejudice of race and class which blinded even church-going youngsters during the week to the truth we sang so sweetly on Sunday: "Jesus loves the little children—all the children of the world."

The local paper reported occasional vandalism but almost no serious crime. No doubt some people did break the Ten Commandments from time to time, but my parents shunned gossip and guilty parties back then didn't flaunt such matters in public. Disciplinary problems at school meant someone was caught chewing gum in class, or maybe a couple was spied kissing or holding hands.

The really rough boys smoked cigarettes and drank beer, the most potent drugs available in Athens, Alabama in those days. Some of the cigarette-smoking and beer-drinking types frequented the soda fountain of the Limestone Drug Store on the courthouse square, a place I walked past when necessary with some trepidation and usually glancing the other way—partly because I thought they looked down on me and partly, to be perfectly honest, because I felt superior to them.

Everything Decent and in Order

The years rolled around in proper seasons, as the trees gave faithful witness. On moonlit January nights, the branches sparkled with icy chandeliers that melted by April into white and pink buds, then turned lush, cool green for July's searing heat, finally exploding into brilliant October reds and yellows and oranges as the days shortened and temperatures fell. The school year followed the agricultural cycles—a short summer recess gave way to six weeks of school, which dismissed again in early fall until the cotton harvest had been picked. Although we lived in town, many of our church friends and schoolmates did not. I joined them in the country and picked cotton to help buy my own clothes at least through junior high years.

My personal world was as stable as the seasons. Daddy went to work every morning and came home again every night.

Mother helped him in the Christian publishing and retail bookstore that was our family business, but she was always home when we got there after school. We never missed a meal at the Fudge table, which, more often than not, also fed someone outside our family—a series of foster children, visiting missionaries, and a host of miscellaneous friends. We didn't have a television, but we had a phonograph and several walls covered with books.

Daddy preached twice every Sunday, a day on which he regularly rose, ate his bowl of Wheaties or Grape Nuts Flakes, then walked the mile to his office to review his sermon. Meanwhile, mother got herself ready, prepared Sunday lunch ("dinner," in those days), then roused, dressed and fed six children, just in time for Daddy to walk back in and announce, "Load up!" That signaled that it was time to go to church, which we did every week whether we wanted to or not.

Mother never complained or suggested any other division of parental labor. We assumed she found as much pleasure in her serving as she provided us through it. I don't remember ever hearing her raise her voice, although one of my more boisterous younger brothers says she did, once. God and Daddy seemed to have the world under control, at least the part I knew anything about. In truth, Mother kept the Fudge household in order, but she did it so unobtrusively we didn't give her the credit.

Daddy Led the Church, and It Was Good

During my younger days, church was about a quarter-mile from our house, which happened also to be my school. Daddy and some of his friends had founded Athens Bible School in 1943, a year before I was born, and the Eastside Church of Christ rented the facilities. Daddy did the preaching and four elders pastored the flock. We respected them then and remember them with affection and esteem to this day. Brother Richter was a butcher and proprietor of Richter's Meat Market downtown. Brother Jarrett was janitor of Athens Bible School. Brother Chandler and Brother Cox were retired.

Under Daddy's enthusiastic tutelage, for which he took no pay, the congregation economized on real estate to devote half its budget to foreign missions. Almost every week, Daddy read the church a report from a missionary in some faraway land, as he constantly encouraged an ever-larger world vision. Each year he attended Bible lectures at several Christian colleges and reported those proceedings to the church the next Sunday he was home. Daddy believed in the "priesthood of all believers" and wanted to pass on to every church member the benefits of his own wider experiences.

We had spiritual disciplines at Eastside, also led by my father. Sunday School began with roll call in each class and you answered by stating how many chapters you had read in the Bible the previous week and whether you had read it every day. As the first order of business when the congregation assembled for worship, Daddy stood beside a large blackboard up front and recorded in precise columns the number of chapters reported by each class and the number of daily Bible readers. He then tallied the columns aloud and grandly announced the final totals.

This exercise provided a running competition against self and one's peers, giving clear incentive and constant reminder of obvious duty. More than once after a week of negligence I remember reading the two short verses of Psalm 117 repeatedly on Saturday night to boost my own report in Sunday School the next morning. Whatever one thinks of the method, motive or process, it is difficult to quarrel with the result: those two majestic verses—and hundreds of others throughout the Bible—were firmly implanted in my youthful mind, hopefully to bear good fruit throughout this life and into the world to come.

"Church" and "change" did not occupy the same sentence in those days. Indeed, church existed in part to ensure that certain things remained the same. We believed that the Bible was true and we were sure that we had correctly deciphered its meaning. It was very difficult for us to understand how other professing Christians ever reached doctrinal conclusions different from ours. "They are either ignorant," some said, "or just plain dishonest." Whatever their problem, our mission was relatively simple: to live by the Bible as best we could, spread correct knowledge to as many others as possible, and protect ourselves from any variations of thinking brought in from outside.

We Sang and Prayed for God's Guidance

We were fundamentalists, although we didn't use that word, and we would no more have read our prayers from a book than we would have lit candles or burned incense. There was an oral tradition, however, and the spontaneous prayers offered Sunday after Sunday turned out practically identical no matter who led them. Looking back now, I realize that this was how the older generation passed to the coming one a detailed and time-honored version of public petition and praise.

The model prayer of my childhood included homage, thanksgiving, and petitions for missionaries on foreign soil, governmental officials, the preacher (for a "ready recollection"), and for "the sick and afflicted." The prayer usually ended by asking God to "guide, guard and direct us" as we went our separate ways into the new week, and to "bring us back together at the next appointed time."

We also frequently sang a hymn titled "Break Thou the Bread of Life" which had us say:

Beyond the sacred page, I seek thee, Lord;
My spirit pants for thee, O living Word!

This presented a certain irony, which passed largely unnoticed, since many of our preachers taught that God never works "separate and apart from the Word."

Even then, the concept of God guiding the individual believer teased my imagination. The fact that I do not remember hearing a single sermon about God's guidance only added to the mystique. What was this divine leading that we sang about and prayed about but never talked about? Naturally God guided, guarded and directed special people in Bible times in wonderful and unexpected ways, but this was the 20th century. We knew that heroes and heroines of both Testaments personally experienced the divine presence in daily life. But they didn't live in Athens, Alabama.

I often wondered, why should God not be just as real to anyone now who also takes him seriously? Could I dare expect specific divine guidance in my own life? These questions frequently came into my mind and would not go away. Did not the Scriptures regularly call him the living God, and distinguish him from dumb idols that neither spoke nor heard nor moved? Didn't the New Testament assure us that Jesus Christ is not dead but alive, that he has all power in heaven and on earth, and that he is the same yesterday, today and forever?

By the time I graduated from high school and went into the world, I desperately wanted to know that God would truly "guide, guard and direct" my life also. Even more than his guidance, I wanted to know the living God himself—to know more than words on a page or in a prayer. I could not comprehend then how involved God already was in my life, through the lives of both my faithful parents. In a real sense, my own story started with each of them.

TO REFLECT OR DISCUSS

1. Can you relate to Edward's particular vision of his childhood? How do environment and culture help shape our individual spiritual and religious experiences?

2. What is your instinctive response to those who say that God's guidance is limited to the Bible itself?

3. When did you first begin to ask God to lead your own life? Do you ever share with others your own testimony concern ing God's faithful guidance?

Chapter 3

From my Mother's Womb

God, give us Christian homes!
Homes where the mother, in queenly quest,
Strives to show others Thy way is best,
Homes where the Lord is an honored guest;
God, give us Christian homes!

–B. B. McKinney

If they tell us anything—those Old Testament stories of Abraham, Isaac and Jacob, of Joseph and Moses and David—they surely say that God directs entire families and nations, even as he guides individual women and men who trust in him. And nothing in the Bible suggests that God desires or expects to be less involved in our families today.

Long before I was born, God was working in two diverse lineages living continents apart—the Shorts in the wilds of Africa, and the Fudges on a farm in Alabama. The two clans would finally merge when Sybil Short and Benjamin ("Bennie") Lee Fudge fell in love, married, and passed their heritage and genes to their six children, of whom I am oldest.

Like King David, whose line included valiant women and men of faith, I look back at my ancestors and praise God for a "goodly heritage." Of course, all those forbears were sinful mortals just like us, but the more I discover about them the more I marvel at how God fashioned such a heritage for my good and his own glory.

Pioneering Land and Gospel

I know little of the Shorts before my great-grandmother. When I was in junior high school, she lived in our town for a while with my missionary grandparents who were on furlough from Africa. She told us stories from her own childhood, of how her pioneer parents loaded all their belongings into a covered wagon and slowly traveled west across the prairies to Kansas where she grew to womanhood. Great-grandmother Short and her husband knew God and walked with him. They passed the faith to their children as well, including my grandfather, William Newton Short, Sr.

Will, as he was known to friends, eventually met and married Delia O'Neal, a strong-willed and able-bodied lass of Scot and Irish blood. In 1921, motivated by a pioneer missionary named McCaleb, they determined to go to India to preach the gospel. When the Indian government refused permission to enter the country, Will and Delia wondered why God allowed this hindrance to their lofty plans, but continued to pray and seek divine guidance.

About that time a pioneer missionary named John Sherriff was visiting in America from the country later called Southern Rhodesia, now Zimbabwe. Originally from New Zealand, he was a stonecutter by trade. As it happened, Mr. Sherriff crossed paths with the young Shorts. When he heard their story he encouraged them to go to Africa instead. "It is clear that God was calling you to the pioneer mission field." he told them. "I believe the door closing to India means he is calling you to Africa instead."

As they continued to pray, Will and Delia felt assured that God was indeed leading them to Rhodesia. And so, like Abraham of old, they said goodbye to all their kin—not knowing if they would ever see them again on earth—and boarded a steamship to Africa, halfway around the world. With their firstborn baby, Foy, they embarked on a faith pilgrimage that would last for life, little knowing then that they would live and labor for more than 60 years on the continent of Africa, broken only by a few visits to the States spaced many years apart.

The Shorts eventually had five children, two sons and three daughters: Foy, Sybil, Beth, Margaret Ann and William Newton, Jr. ("Bill"). The love for Africa and its people continued in the Short children. After graduating from Abilene Christian College and helping start Athens Bible School alongside my father, Foy and his wife Margaret returned to Africa where they served until the 1990's.

Beth married Henry Ewing, whom she met at Abilene Christian, and they returned to Africa for many years until Henry contracted terminal cancer and returned to the United States, where he died. Beth served God for several years in Amarillo, Texas after Henry's death. Then, in her late sixties and legally blind with acute glaucoma, she returned to Tanzania in East Africa. There she ministered in a medical mission, where wild game provided the only fresh meat and the nearest telephone was 40 miles away. "My days are busy, exciting and full of joy," she typically reported, "except for the times when Satan tells me I am tired, discouraged, and lonely. That is the battle of every Christian in every country, living in any circumstance, isn't it? Just remember, the victory is in Jesus."

My parents also planned to go to Africa when they married, but again God had other plans. Mother eventually returned to Rhodesia after my father died, and cared for her own aged parents during their final years. While she was there, my youngest brother Paul and his wife also moved to preach in Rhodesia, where their two sons were born.

Preacher, Carpenter and Medicine Man

Though Rhodesia was part of the British Empire, the comforts and conveniences of western civilization did not extend to the

rural area where my mother grew up. At first, her family occupied a one-room mud hut with a dirt floor and a thatched roof.
Later, Will made bricks from clay, fired them in a kiln he built
himself, and erected a permanent house. Like the American pio-
neers, the Shorts had to rely on whatever was at hand during
their early years in Africa, making only two trips to town each
year for flour, sugar, salt and other staples.

Besides being a preacher and teacher, Will Short was also a
medicine man of sorts—administering first-aid to tribes-people for
whom the simplest antiseptics seemed almost magical. Sybil still
recalls the excitement at home when the Tonga villagers, in a great
state of panic, came carrying a young woman named Vundu. Her
arm had been bitten off by a crocodile, they explained, as she
washed her clothes in the river. Using what he had at hand, Sybil's
father fashioned a tourniquet to stop the bleeding and poured a
bottle of hydrogen peroxide to disinfect the wound.

It was clear that Vundu would quickly die without medical
attention, and the nearest medical facility was over 50 miles
away. There were no highways, and the nearest railway track
was miles from the mission compound. In her weakened state
Vundu could not walk, but her fellow tribes-people refused to
carry her unless they were paid. So Will hired the woman's relatives to carry her to the railroad where they flagged a train. Soon
she was off to the hospital while he and his wife remained
behind to pray.

By God's grace, Vundu survived and regained strength,
though without one arm. That raised an additional problem, however. Because of the handicap, the Tongans considered Vundu
unable to function as a wife and mother, making her an outcast
from the village. When Will and Delia learned of Vundu's plight,
they hired her as a nurse-maid for their own younger children, a
post she faithfully fulfilled for many years.

Although human neighbors were few, the Shorts had plenty
of non-human companions. Each evening, lacking screens for

windows or doors, Delia wrapped her children's arms and legs in sheets like mummies to protect them from malaria-bearing mosquitoes until she tucked them into net-covered cots for the night. Night in the African bush was far different from night in a typical American city. As the Psalmist says, when man goes home from his labor, the animals go out seeking prey. At night the Shorts listened from inside their hut as lions, leopards and other creatures prowled about outside. They frequently found a variety of snakes inside the house as well.

The family's gardens were especially attractive to large baboons. These dangerous animals preferred to steal the family's food rather than forage for themselves. Sybil remembers the time her father surprised a large male baboon raiding the garden and shot it. The beast fled, only wounded. Knowing the threat a wounded wild animal poses to others, Will tracked it into the hills with his gun and his beloved Great Dane. Suddenly the baboon appeared from the brush and attacked Will. Without hesitation, the dog leaped to protect his master. With one savage bite the huge baboon killed the dog before Will could finally destroy the baboon.

The Shorts also encountered adversity of a more ominous nature. Although they brought good news of Jesus, not all the Africans were eager to hear such news. Particularly hostile were the witchdoctors, who, like Simon the Sorcerer in the Book of Acts, found pleasure in exercising control over the Tonga and Shona villagers. If a villager dared to defy the witchdoctor, the witchdoctor cast a spell on him or her and predicted the villager's death on a certain future day. Whether through demonic power, psycho-suggestion, or some other force, the witchdoctor's prediction frequently came to pass. Understandably, the villagers feared such power and hesitated to resist the witchdoctor s authority.

Will told the villagers that God's Son had come to earth and died for their sins. Like people in every nation, they should renounce all evil practices and serve Jesus as Lord of their lives. Such teaching directly challenged the witchdoctor's fierce authority, and he sternly threatened to cast a fatal spell on any African who accepted Jesus as Savior and Lord.

"What should we do?" the believing Africans asked Will Short. "Dare we go against the witchdoctor? We have seen the strength of his spells before. His magic is very powerful!"

"The witchdoctor is only a man, just like you and me," he replied. "Any power he possesses comes from evil spirits. But Jesus is stronger than all evil spirits—in fact, Jesus has done personal battle with Satan, the chief of evil spirits, and has defeated him. We know that is true because Jesus rose from the dead. He is living today and he will live forever. Do not be afraid to defy the witchdoctor by following Jesus as Lord. Jesus' power is greater than any magic the witchdoctor might possess." And, more than 60 years later, Will Short could say he never heard of a Christian believer who died for defying a witchdoctor.

Learning Early to Depend on God

Besides preaching and teaching in person, Grandfather Short also wrote and published thousands of pages of gospel literature and Christian materials during his sixty years in Rhodesia. He set the type by hand, one letter at a time, then reproduced it on an archaic hand-fed press that printed one sheet at a time. He also edited and published a gospel magazine called *Rays of Light.*

Delia Short taught Sybil and her other children until about seventh grade. Then they were old enough, according to British custom, to leave home and go away to boarding school. After completing boarding school, my mother and her sister Beth left home again, this time aboard a steamship to attend college in America. Their home-schooling provided a solid foundation. When Mother took her college entrance exams, the school officials informed her that she qualified to begin college as a junior! God's protection over the two Short girls was also evident in their safe passage across the Atlantic. The very ship that brought them to America was sent to the ocean bottom by German torpedoes on its next voyage.

Sybil learned at an early age to depend on God for daily necessities. The Shorts had scarcely settled in Africa when the U.S. suffered the Great Depression of the 20's and 30's. If the supporting churches back home had no money, there was also none to send to missionaries in Africa. When that happened, Will homesteaded 3,000 acres of farmland. Growers around him raised tobacco, but Will considered it improper to sell to others something he shunned himself, so he raised mealies (corn) instead. The whole family helped as each could. Will built an ox-wagon for Foy, then a young teenager, who drove it behind 16 oxen across dozens of roadless miles to take mealies to the railroad for market.

Other difficulties were human in origin. Will Short believed the Bible to be God's Word, and he regarded its teaching of utmost importance. If he concluded that something was taught in Scripture, he stood on that—regardless of what anyone else thought about it. This got him in trouble more than once, including a period during the 1930's and 1940's when some United States preachers decided to stamp out of the Churches of Christ a particular interpretation of Revelation known as premillennialism. That view says that Jesus will return to earth before a golden age of 1,000 years known as the Millennium, during which he will personally reign over the entire world in perfect justice and peace.

This campaign of extermination included personal attacks on anyone suspected of holding the forbidden view, demanding their resignations as preachers, teachers or missionaries when possible, smearing their reputations by well-placed rumors and reports, boycotting their church-related businesses, and even burning books and hymnals thought to contain heretical notions.

During that frenzy, someone in the U.S. accused one of Will Short's fellow missionaries of believing in premillennialism. The zealots decided that Short should disown his friend and denounce him as a heretic. Will Short was not premillennial in his own interpretation of Scripture. However, he did not consider the final details of world history to be nearly so important as trusting in Jesus and treating each other with Christian love and respect today. He therefore refused to disown the accused brother.

By refusing to follow their counsel, Will consciously defied the authority of the purge-leaders. The zealots responded by contacting churches that financially assisted Will and Delia Short in Africa, and urging them to stop all support immediately. Many followed this advice, requiring Will to curtail his preaching temporarily and find other ways to provide his family's needs.

He commuted to Salisbury in Southern Rhodesia for a time, where he worked as a brick mason during the week and returned to his family each weekend. Later he made large ox wagons, entirely from hand. My mother remembers carving spokes for the wagon wheels, then watching her father as he put iron rims around the spokes and heated the rims to shrink them into place.

A Peaceful and Holy Death

Will Short was a man of deep piety and strong personal faith in God. He knew God not as a doctrinal topic but as father, companion and ever-faithful friend. He prayed hard and he looked for answers. Many times he saw God answer prayers in extraordinary ways.

God honored this lifelong friendship in a special way when the time came for Granddaddy to die. One day in his 80's, Will Short went into his bedroom as he always did after breakfast to read his Bible and pray. When he didn't come out after a long time, a nurse went in to check on him. There he sat, head bowed, Bible in his lap, as if in prayer. Like Enoch of old, he walked with God. This day it was as if God said to him, "We're closer to my house than we are to yours: just come on home with me."

Mother's Quiet Strength

My mother followed her parents' godly example, and she attempted to instill the same piety in her six children. Like Will,

Sybil Short manifests a quiet spirit. Though soft-spoken in voice, however, her influence rang loud and clear as she first modeled then molded us in piety and responsibility.

Although she usually remained in the background, in keeping with the customs and expectations of the time and place, she has always actively promoted the Kingdom of God. Not only did she raise six children—doing so singlehandedly insofar as daily, hands-on details—she also opened her heart and house to seven or eight other children who needed a home for varying periods of time.

Her public ministry included teaching a popular, weekly ladies Bible class for many years. And, though her conscience compelled her to remain silent in public worship, she also authored a Sunday School workbook on the Book of Isaiah which was widely used by adult classes composed of both men and women.

Since Daddy considered television a waste of time (even in the 1950's), we read for entertainment and for information. Mother kept us supplied with inspirational and devotional materials. She still carries on this ministry to her children today, although all now have children of their own and are scattered from Florida to California. Her letters, e-mails and conversations regularly talk about the heavenly Father. God is very real to Mother, having accompanied her through many difficult circumstances. The Heavenly Father remains her constant companion now as she approaches her 80's, devotedly caring for her second husband, Joe, in Ohio. She is the epitome of the worthy woman described in Proverbs 31.

TO REFLECT OR DISCUSS

1. How would you describe the faith of someone who leaves the comforts of home and family to take the gospel to a distant and undeveloped country?

2. What were or are your mother's greatest influences on your life? If you are a mother, how would you most like your children to remember you?

3. Think of specific character traits that Jacob, Samuel, Jesus and Timothy might have remembered about their own mothers.

Chapter 4

And in my Father's Image

Faith of our fathers! we will love
Both friend and foe in all our strife;
And preach thee, too, as love knows how,
By kindly words and virtuous life.

–Frederick W. Faber

There have been Fudges since at least the 12th or 13th century in England. Although I cannot prove it, I am confident that my ancestor Jacob Fudge, Sr., born in 1723 in the American Colony of Pennsylvania, descended from the British Fudges.

Patriots, Planters and Johnny Rebs

Although Jacob received three land grants from King George III, he was an American patriot who fought for independence in the Revolutionary War. He later moved his wife and nine children to Indian country in South Carolina. There he owned both land and slaves. I do not know the details of Jacob's religion or the extent of his piety. However, his last will and testament indicates that he was a Christian believer, if not an outstanding speller. As he faced death in 1789, he wrote:

> In the name of God, Amen, I Jacob Fudge Senior of South
> Carolina and Edgefield County, being weak in body but of

erfect mind and memory thanks be given unto God. Calling unto mind the mortallity of my body and knowing that it is appointed for all men once to die, do make and ordain this My Last Will and Testament....I gave and recommend my soul unto the Hands of Almighty God that gave it, and my body I recommend to the Earth to be buryed in a decent Christian Buryal at the Discretion of my Executors, Nothing doubting but at the General Resurrection I shall receive the same again By the mighty power of God.

William, the third of Jacob's five sons, began his own family in South Carolina. Sometime between 1800 and 1810, he migrated west to Limestone County in North Alabama. There he reared his son Solomon, and established roots that continue until this day. Solomon begat seven children, as the Bible puts it. The sixth was William Henry Fudge.

When the Civil War erupted, William Henry enlisted in the 35th Alabama Infantry, Confederate Company "G". He was captured by General Sherman, held as a prisoner of war, and released on Independence Day of 1861. Still passionate for the Confederate cause, he soon re-enlisted and fought at the Battle of Shiloh. William Henry Fudge had six children. His oldest was born in 1864 as the war raged and the South burned. William Henry named him Edward Benjamin Lee, the "Lee" bestowed in honor of the beloved Southern general, Robert E. Lee.

His parents may have named him Edward Benjamin Lee Fudge, but the neighbors called him "Ed." In time, Ed Fudge married Susie Smith, who was about 30 years younger. She taught him to read after they married, using the *King James Bible* as a primer. They had eight children, my father being the oldest of the brood. Ed Fudge's household was poor but always devout.

Ed operated a gristmill for a time and also ran a country store. Mostly, however, he farmed, as a sharecropper on other people's land. I remember visiting my Fudge grandparents as a preschool youngster. They lived in a small wooden house in the country, unpainted, with an empty thread spool for a doorknob. Grandpa Fudge had long whiskers, wore overalls, and frightened me without knowing it or intending to. He and Grandma Fudge both died before I started school.

Bennie Lee Fudge: A Little Man with Big Ambitions

My father, Benjamin ("Bennie") Lee, was born on April 5, 1914, when Ed was 50 years old. Bennie Lee weighed in prematurely at a fragile 3-1/2 pounds. Susie wrapped him in a piece of wool blanket and gently laid him in a shoebox. She then positioned the shoe box near the wood stove in the kitchen, the warmest place in the house, and asked God to spare her firstborn. God answered her prayers for that baby's survival. Thirty years later, Susie's baby, now a father, would keep vigil all night over his own premature firstborn son, beseeching God to save my life, even as his own life had once been spared.

Bennie Lee never grew to be large, but he made up for it in determination and tenacity. As a young teen, he watched some older boys jump over a huge log that had fallen in the forest. Bennie Lee tried to jump the log also, but fell short, breaking his leg. The leg was in a cast for six weeks. When the cast was finally removed, Bennie Lee's first order of business was to go jump that log. People did not always agree with his judgment but few ever doubted his determination.

To rural families in those days, large families meant more hands for necessary labor, of which there was always plenty to go around. When my father was 14, Grandpa Fudge was disabled, and young Bennie Lee assumed additional responsibility as the oldest able-bodied man of the house. For the next 15 years, he and his younger brothers alternated going to school and farming to support the family.

Since the family could not afford a tractor, even if one had been available, Bennie Lee plowed with mules. An earnest student

of the Scriptures, he often carried his Bible into the fields, reading it whenever the mules rested. He considered the Bible to be
his governing authority, and he eagerly digested its contents from
start to finish. From the book of Philippians he took a lifetime
motto: "I can do all things through Christ who strengthens me."
Alongside that Scripture, he frequently quoted another, unin-
spired saying: "It's amazing what one man can accomplish if he
doesn't care who gets the credit!" Early on, Bennie Lee dedicated
his life to God's service with little thought of personal credit, or
glory for the results of his faithful service.

The fields also provided his first pulpit. At age 20, still farming
to support the family, Bennie Lee often practiced sermons while he
plowed. Soon he began to receive invitations to speak at nearby
churches. More than once, neighbors who happened past the
fields reported hearing Bennie Lee preaching to the stumps and to
the mules.

Daddy graduated from high school at age 21, worked a few
more years to support the family, then went to Nashville,
Tennessee to attend David Lipscomb College. To earn his keep, he
cleaned campus buildings at night and did other odd jobs. A
teacher at heart, he savored the academic environment, but he was
particularly inspired by the college president E. H. Ijams, a godly
man, deeply committed to Jesus Christ and absolutely uncon-
cerned with personal advancement or church politics.

David Lipscomb was then a junior college, so after finishing
courses there, Bennie Lee traveled to far-away Texas to complete
his bachelor's degree at Abilene Christian College (now
University). He majored in Greek, the original language of the
New Testament. There he also met Sybil Short, who at age 17 had
journeyed even farther—from Africa. Their initial impressions of
each other were a study in contrasts. After their first date Bennie
Lee told his roommate, "If Miss Short was not determined to go
to Africa, I'd marry her." He did not know that before their date
Sybil had told her roommate, "I wouldn't marry him if he were

the last man on earth." But she later changed her mind and married him anyway.

They Thought Africa, But God Said No

Bennie Lee and Sybil planned to finish college, marry, then return to Africa as missionaries—after Bennie Lee had fulfilled another longstanding dream. First, he intended to found Athens Bible School, a private institution in his Alabama home town, where students could study the Bible every day alongside their regular academic classes, and whose administration and faculty would consciously seek to instill Christian principles and values in their students.

The vision became reality in 1943 when Athens Bible School opened its doors with grades 7-12, adding lower grades thereafter year by year. The African dream was not to be fulfilled, as the same God who led Will and Delia's path to that continent now turned Bennie Lee and Sybil's path away from it.

My parents graduated from Abilene Christian College in 1943, married the next evening, and moved to Rogersville, Alabama, a village about 20 miles west of Athens. There they lived for about four years, where my father preached for the local Church of Christ, before moving to Athens to be closer to the new school.

Although he never made it to Africa in person, Bennie Lee was destined to become a world evangelist while remaining in Athens, Alabama, through the pulpit of the printed page. "Twenty-six lead soldiers," my father called the alphabet, "soldiers that can conquer the world!" It began as a simple book-rack at Athens Bible School, where students, staff or visitors could purchase any of a handful of basic Bibles or study tools. Soon, however, it grew into a small business, clearly destined to become an independent bookstore—if someone felt called into that ministry.

Bennie Lee felt called. Under his enthusiastic and untiring leadership, the fledgling business kept expanding until its heyday when it included four retail stores, a publishing arm, a dealership division and a direct sales force that hired college students to sell Bibles and other books door-to-door during summers. Bennie Lee named his business to reflect its purpose: Christian Education Institute, or "C.E.I." for short. After its ministry expanded world-wide, he kept the same initials but chose the corporate name of Christian Enterprises International.

When Bennie Lee was growing up, Sunday Schools in most Churches of Christ used literature called "the Quarterly." Bennie Lee noticed that the Quarterly contained very few actual Scripture quotations, and that a pupil could complete all its exercises with-out ever having to open a Bible at all. "Why," he reckoned, "a student could attend Sunday School for years with this material, and never use a Bible!" He believed that Sunday School pupils ought to have more, and that with God's help he could provide it.

So he bought a variety of public school books for each grade level and immersed himself in them until he felt comfortable with the respective vocabularies and styles. Then he went away to a nearby town where he should not be disturbed, checked into a hotel, and wrote a series of Sunday School literature for all ages. Students growing up with his material progressed through the Bible time after time, beginning with a broad sweep of major childhood stories, gradually deepening the content through repeated cycles.

Bennie Lee called his series the "Use Your Bible" workbooks, and anyone using this literature did exactly that! Each lesson con-tained true/false questions, matching questions, fill-in-the-blanks and other type quizzes, usually requiring the student to read three or four chapters of the Bible through for each exercise. A generation or two of youngsters in the Churches of Christ and Independent Christian Churches grew up on these workbooks—many of them thinking that "Bennie Lee Fudge" was a woman. Sybil, who was an accomplished artist, illustrated the workbooks as Bennie Lee wrote them.

Besides his Sunday School workbooks, Bennie Lee also published gospel booklets, children's Bible songs, a history of missionaries sent out by Churches of Christ and assorted other works. Over the years, some of this material was translated and published in Spanish and Norwegian as well as several languages of Africa and the Philippines. Meanwhile, the English editions found their way throughout the world.

Scholar and Counselor to the Multitudes

While still a young adult, Bennie Lee also began a daily radio program over station WJMW in Athens, a cooperative effort of the Churches of Christ of Limestone County. The program was called "Spiritual Guidance," and it started with different speakers each month. During one of Bennie Lee's first months, a listener wrote him a letter asking several Bible questions, which Bennie Lee answered on the program. Soon other listeners sent in questions. Bennie Lee kept answering—and his audience kept asking—for the next 30 years.

It was my boyhood thrill to accompany Daddy to the radio station for his program shortly after noon. The rule was that I could sit at the studio table with the large microphone in the center, but I could not talk. If a cough or sneeze arose which could not be suppressed, there was a dime-size button one could push to temporarily deaden the mike.

In memory I still hear the announcer's ringing introduction: "The time now is 12:15," he began. "Each week day at this same time, the Churches of Christ of Limestone County present 15 minutes of spiritual guidance. The Churches of Christ and their ministers are always ready to help you with your problems of Bible study and Christian living. Your speaker today, and your regular speaker on the program, is Brother Bennie Lee Fudge. Brother Fudge." At that cue, the red light bulb outside our studio flashed on, Daddy quickly cleared his throat and said, "Thank you, Bob, and good afternoon everyone!"

As Bennie Lee's reputation as a biblical scholar and practical Christian counselor spread, his bookstore on the courthouse square became a haven for visitors from far and near. Because such welcomed distractions took much of his time during the day, Bennie Lee often walked the mile from his house to the office after the evening meal, then toiled there until midnight or beyond on his publishing business.

Every Sunday Bennie Lee ministered at some local church, serving a succession of congregations through the years. Wherever he served, he promoted world missions, preached expository sermons and usually taught a Sunday School class, often of teenagers. He was a master storyteller who enchanted children and kept their parents spellbound as well.

Conviction Despite the Consequences

Throughout his life, Bennie Lee taught the Bible as he saw it, without regard to popularity or financial consequences. While still on the farm, he had concluded through his own study that Christians should not kill in the service of their country in time of war. The conviction grew firmer while he was at David Lipscomb College, a school whose namesake founder had urged complete disassociation from civil governments except to pay taxes as Jesus commanded.

In keeping with this line of thought, Bennie Lee never voted, although he was keenly interested in political issues throughout his life. While still in college at Abilene, in the midst of World War II, he wrote a booklet setting out his conscientious objector views. This stand was highly unpopular under the circumstances and earned him the scorn and censure of many. Although he did not enjoy being criticized, he never flinched or backed down when conscience compelled a course of conduct or teaching.

During the 1950's, the Churches of Christ—and many individual families that composed them—divided over the way various evangelistic and benevolent works should be organized. One group believed that Scripture required congregations to support missionaries directly, without any intervening organization or coordinating congregation. The mainstream majority concluded that the Bible allowed diversity in such matters. Some people of both opinions discovered in this controversy an opportunity to advance their personal and partisan interests—even if it meant hurting others in the process.

A favorite forum for discussion was the public debate, which pitted advocates of both sides against each other and usually generated more heat than light. Although Bennie Lee had been a regional fundraiser for one of the evangelistic programs involved, he decided after one such debate that the opposition side was correct. Naturally, he notified the program's sponsors that he could no longer support their activity. When the program's sponsors learned this, they issued an ultimatum. "You may do as you please," they told Bennie Lee, "but be aware that if you persist in this viewpoint, it will be our duty as we travel throughout the nation to warn all 'faithful' churches not to order their Sunday School supplies from your 'anti' business."

Such threats only stiffened the convictions Bennie Lee had already formed. When it became evident that he would not budge, his adversaries did as they had warned and led a national boycott against his publishing company, ultimately forcing it into involuntary bankruptcy. Bennie Lee accepted all this as the price of conscience, however, and never complained or sought revenge. Nor did he draw lines of fellowship with those who persecuted him. "I'll fellowship you as long as you will let me," was his attitude. He remained an enigma to many, who could not understand how one so rigid in his own opinions could warmly embrace others who sincerely disagreed with those opinions.

Vision Beyond Sectarian Boundaries

For many years, Bennie Lee also edited a magazine called *Gospel Digest*, a Christian journal patterned after *Reader's Digest*.

During my childhood and youth, he subscribed to every paper published in English by any branch of our religious movement known to him throughout the world. He also received and avidly read many other papers from various people completely separate from our particular movement.

He encouraged others to have the same spirit of inquiry and open mind. When I was a teenager, I studied (and vigorously debated with) religious correspondence courses published by Seventh-day Adventists, the Catholic Knights of Columbus, Herbert W. Armstrong's Worldwide Church of God, and other groups. Daddy encouraged me to critique material for myself. While he was always watching nearby, ready to answer questions, he never gave the impression that he was standing over my shoulder or imposing his own conclusions on me. "Study the Bible for yourself," he always encouraged, "and stand firmly on whatever you find that it teaches."

To be fair, most preachers I knew talked that way. The difference between many of them and my father was that he really meant it—and he expected us to do the same. That honest search for truth later led me to some conclusions with which my father, if living, would likely disagree. Occasionally, someone who knew his particular convictions confronts me by asking what my father would think of my own, different views. Without hesitation, I tell them that he would endorse my efforts to understand God's Word for myself and would insist that I stand firm on my own convictions. In fact, that is what he taught me to do—by his word and also by his example.

Unlike many others in his religious fellowship, Bennie Lee regarded all immersed believers as brothers and sisters in Christ, whether they were connected with the Churches of Christ or not. When he died in February of 1972, more than 700 mourners attended his memorial service, and a cross-section of the community called on the family to express esteem for the man they all called "Brother Fudge."

A Heart Full of Compassion

Daddy found it almost impossible to express emotion. When he took me to college 650 miles from home, he unloaded my suitcases and gave me $30.00, which was all the money he had with him. Then, rather than hugging me, as I would do with my own children, he extended his hand and said, "Well, see you in the funny papers." Then he got in his car and drove away. Years later, my mother said he had told her it was the hardest thing he had ever done, and that he had to leave quickly before I saw him cry.

Yet he was one of the most tenderhearted men I have ever known. Many times I saw him buy shoes, or clothes or food for some needy family or individual. Every Sunday afternoon for many years, he and Mother called on a dear Christian sister who was confined to bed with a paralyzing disease, to read a chapter from the Bible and then to pray. "We go to encourage Mrs. Jarrett," Daddy often observed, "but every time she encourages us instead."

Then there was Sam, a bewhiskered, toothless and handicapped man who operated a state-subsidized concession stand on the corner next to Daddy's bookstore and resided in the old town hotel. Sam felt he couldn't go to church, but he read his Bible regularly. Every Christmas, my father gave Sam an *Annual Sunday School Lesson Commentary* for the following year. "God can take care of Sam," he once told me, "and I am sure he understands why Sam does not attend church." No Christmas or Thanksgiving meal was complete at our house until we prepared a plate for Sam, which Daddy seemed to take great pleasure in delivering personally.

When Daddy died, Sam trudged a mile in freezing weather, hobbling on his cane, to pay respects to his old friend. A few years later, I had the honor of speaking at Sam's funeral. The Lord only knows for sure, of course, but I encouraged those present to believe that God had taken care of Sam after all.

Forgiving as Christ Forgave

Because he knew God's forgiveness, Daddy also forgave others who wronged him. Since childhood, Daddy had aspired to serve as an elder in a local church. Although he preached for many years, he never had that privilege. Two years before Daddy died, his congregation nominated him for its eldership. Because of Daddy's recent business bankruptcy, however, another preacher in town, who did not belong to that congregation, protested the nomination and it was withdrawn. Daddy's lifelong dream was crushed, and his spirit was crushed with it. However, he never complained or threatened to get even with the man who had hurt him.

About a year later, the telephone rang one evening as we finished dinner, and the caller asked for Daddy. It was an elder of another congregation in the county, about to employ a new preacher. "We are thinking of hiring Brother So-and-So," the caller said, referring to the man who had killed Daddy's dream a year before. "We know you know him, and we would appreciate your opinion of his qualifications."

Without hesitation, Daddy replied. "He is a good man, and I think he will do an excellent job for you," he said. "I hope you will offer him the position." He hung up the receiver and sat back down.

The rest of us were mute with astonishment. "How could you say that?" we finally asked. "Don't you remember what he did to you?"

"What?"

We reminded him of the earlier incident.

"Well," he said, "I had completely forgotten that. But even if I had remembered it, I would have said the same thing because it was true and he will do a good job for that church."

Modeling Priorities and Values

Perhaps most of all, Daddy instilled in his children a strong sense of priorities. A conversation shortly before he died will live forever in my memory. Each Christmas, Daddy invited us family members to an official, if informal, business meeting. It was a legal requirement for the various corporations of the family business, but it was more. Daddy also used the occasion to reflect on the past year and to sketch his vision of the year just ahead.

The scene was Christmas 1971. Though we did not know it then, it would be Daddy's last Christmas on this earth. He had built a cherished business—a life ministry—and he had seen it crumble before his eyes. He was just beginning to rebuild from the ashes, as it were. There was little reason for excitement it seemed, and perhaps much cause for sorrow.

After the formal corporate necessities of the family business meeting were completed, Daddy took a sheet of paper from his pocket. "I have some wonderful news," he exclaimed excitedly. "I have recently re-read all the major books on successful living known to me. From them I have compiled a list of the ten most important things in life. I am delighted to tell you today that I have nine of those ten. What is more, the only one I lack is money—and it is at the bottom of the list! " Six weeks later he was dead at age 57, struck down by pneumonia within seven days from apparent good health. But the values and priorities he modeled will live in my heart forever.

Once he returned from college, Bennie Lee Fudge never lived outside northern Alabama, whose rich red soil his ancestors had tilled for more than a century. But in the providence of God, this boy who once preached to the stumps and to his crops lived to spread the gospel by printed page to continents and islands around the world. True to his slogan, he didn't care who got the credit, and only God knows the full measure of his accomplishments.

This was the home and the environment into which, by the sovereign leading of God, I was privileged to be born.

TO REFLECT OR DISCUSS

1. Edward's father obviously influenced him in many ways. How has your father influenced you for good?

2. If you are a father, how would you like for your children to remember you?

3. How does the example of earthly parents help or hinder their children's understanding of God as our heavenly Father?

Chapter 5

The Normative, Written Scriptures

Thy word is everlasting truth;
How pure is every page!
That holy book shall guide our youth,
And well support our age.

–Isaac Watts

Like my father, I was also born too soon—at least six weeks by ordinary calculations. I arrived by Caesarean section, the agonizing conclusion of Mother's difficult first pregnancy, of which she spent the final eight weeks lying on her back in a hospital bed at Dr. Jackson's Clinic.

One should not imagine a modern metropolitan hospital when picturing Dr. Jackson's establishment. This single-doctor facility fulfilled the vow of David E. Jackson, an earnest country boy who once promised his neighbors that if they would pay for his medical education he would return to the community after graduation and serve their families for the rest of his life.

The clinic sat on a hilltop 20 miles outside Athens, Alabama, across the road from a rambling, multi-purpose building that served as service station, grocery store and United States Post Office—the entire business district of Lester, Alabama. Inside the hospital babies cried, children huddled close to their mothers and the pungent smell of ether permeated the air. Outside, rows of cotton stalks covered with hard, green bolls waited to unfold their fluffy contents to the autumnal sun, while brown and white cows grazed on green grass as far as the eye could see.

Although fearfully and wonderfully made, I was definitely unfinished on July 13, 1944. Divine providence and the physician's wisdom decided to complete my formation in the primitive incubator that passed as an artificial womb. When I was unable to digest nourishment, my father prayed all night for God to spare my life and the Lord mercifully answered his prayer. I finally went home at age six weeks and began attending church the following Sunday. Even as a miniature worshiper quite unaware of my surroundings, my spiritual training had begun.

From Infancy, the Holy Scriptures

Some of my earliest memories are of Sunday School. "What's this?" the teacher would ask, holding up her Bible. "The Bi-ble!" a dozen little Alabama voices chimed in response. Cheered by the correct answer, the teacher would venture to ask: "And whose word is it?"

"God's!" the conscientious preschoolers replied. "Good," she said. "And we have a song about that this morning. It goes like this:

> O, the B-l-B-L-E;
> Yes, that's the book for me;
> I stand alone on the Word of God,
> the B-I-B-L-E."

When I was about four years old, my father decided to teach me to read—both the English we spoke, and the Greek of the New Testament. Two years before I started to school I was drilling over the alphabet and, alongside it, the "Alpha, Beta" from which the word is derived. Unfortunately, Daddy's work demands cut short our classes, perhaps nipping a classical career in the bud. Greek had to wait until college 14 years later.

But the biblical education continued. Each evening for many years, Daddy conducted family devotions around the dinner table. When the meal was completed, Mother, or a child whose turn it was, removed the dishes and Daddy fetched from his study a stack of Bibles of various translations and distributed them around the table. He then read three chapters aloud—except on Sundays, when he read five—and we followed along in whatever version we happened to have. Then Daddy led an evening prayer. This plan carried us through the Bible in one year. The next year, Daddy selected a different translation to read aloud and we repeated the process.

Athens Bible School

In the Fall of 1950, I enrolled in first grade at Athens Bible School, popularly known as "ABS," and continued there until I graduated from high school in the Spring of 1962. We attended a Bible class every school day, and a daily chapel service as well. Elementary school chapel emphasized Bible drills, while speakers addressing grades 7-12 rehearsed the lives of biblical characters to implant practical attitudes and morality.

The Joseph story from the Book of Genesis especially inspired me. "Keep God first in your life," it showed so plainly, "and he will always be with you, no matter what others may do and regardless of the circumstances which life unfolds." Some chapel speaker also lifted a seed from the tale of this ancient dreamer and planted a dream in my heart. "God always sees you and knows you," he said, "however insignificant you may feel, and he will go before you to open doors of opportunity if you will trust and follow him."

During those 12 years at ABS we plausibly memorized every biblical fact one can pack into a list. By fourth grade, I could recite from memory the 66 books of the Bible, Jacob's 12 sons (and one daughter), Jesus' 12 Apostles, the ten plagues, the 15 judges of Israel, all the kings of Israel and of Judah, and Luke's register of the generations from Adam to Jesus.

By the time we finished elementary school, we might not know our way to the adjoining county, but we knew the route from Egypt to the Promised Land. We couldn't recite the Gettysburg Address, but we could stand and say the Beatitudes, the fruit of the Spirit, the works of the flesh and the Christian graces of Second Peter without missing a beat. We learned to quote select verses and chapters from the *King James Version* of the Bible, until our repertoire included Psalms 1, 8, 15, 23, 24 and 100, as well as the Nativity story from the Gospel According to Luke and the Sermon on the Mount.

This intensive biblical training had fringe benefits. Irven Lee, my fifth grade Bible teacher, took several of us on tours to area congregations, where we dramatically exhibited the benefits of a "Christian education." We sat on the front pew while Brother Lee (as everyone called him) drilled us on Bible facts to the amazement of these North Alabama churches. It was an impressive spectacle, since few adults present could match our prowess at recalling sacred data.

When we had sufficiently wowed the audience with holy details, we changed mental gears to Bible geography and awed them some more. With a sweep of his hand in the air, Brother Lee drew an imaginary Mediterranean shoreline representing the coastline of Palestine, and we named the provinces, towns, rivers and mountains where the Bible stories actually transpired.

As we moved into adolescence, ABS stressed our "four-way growth"—intellectual, physical, social and spiritual. Like Jesus, we hoped to "increase in wisdom and stature and in favor with God and man." Rules sprang up like mushrooms to fit every new situation. Upon inquiry, they were defended as having "always been the policy of this school." The card game Rook was okay for entertainment, but real "playing cards"—also known as "spot cards"—were forbidden, since they were associated with gambling. Hollywood movies were also prohibited because of their evil influence, and anyone caught attending the "picture show" risked disciplinary action. But the area that inspired greatest concern involved sexuality.

In our world, it was an uncontested fact that physical contact between boys and girls often led to fornication, and the *King James Bible* clearly admonished: "it is good for a man not to touch a woman." In their wisdom, therefore, the authorities determined that we should avoid touching the opposite sex.

That meant sitting on opposite sides of the bus on official school trips, with interior lights remaining lit to prevent trespassing. It also meant no close dancing—or any other kind for that matter—since dancing had the "appearance of evil." Roller-skating at the town rink was a borderline activity, because boys and girls often held hands or even embraced while skating, which God might possibly regard as dancing. Naturally the opposite sexes were forbidden to swim together—"mixed bathing" it was called—since, again, one thing might lead to another.

The deciders of such things certainly meant well, no doubt about that. At the same time, many of their human prohibitions only intensified the attractiveness of the forbidden. Some would even suggest that this strict regimen warped our normal psychological development in the long term. But enough of that. I have wandered from the point.

Our indoctrination, in the literal and best sense of the word, culminated in A. J. Rollings' 12th grade Bible class. Legendary for a couple of generations in those parts, Brother Rollings' Bible class required us to memorize some 1,200 verses of Scripture on a wide assortment of subjects from throughout the Bible. To some students, the class loomed as a final hurdle they must overcome to graduate. I was among others who savored it then and still continue to draw from it today, these 40 years later.

That affection was for the teacher as much as for the subject. Like the country parson in Oliver Goldsmith's poem "Deserted Village," one of Brother Rollings' favorite works, it could also be said of him that "truth from his lips prevailed with double sway;

and fools, who came to mock, remained to pray."

Teaching at ABS was a sideline for Brother Rollings, who began preaching for the downtown Market Street Church of Christ at age 27 and continued until age 69. During those years he married, buried or otherwise prayed over representatives of most families of the 52 Churches of Christ in Limestone County, Alabama, and a great many other believers and unbelievers besides. He had been raised in the mountains of East Tennessee by a widowed father who, though relatively unschooled, was an intellectual genius and a veritable walking encyclopedia. The whole world was his classroom; the time-honored body of great literature was his source for personal wisdom and inspiration.

A. J. Rollings carried on his father's tradition. His own preaching, like his teaching, consisted primarily of quotations from Scripture and famous poems, illustrated by anecdotes from the Bible and *Reader's Digest*, all aimed at basic Christian living and expressed with clarity and simplicity.

Totally unselfconscious, he wept openly without shame when so moved. If he met you on the post office steps and discovered some spiritual need, he instinctively put his arm around your shoulder, bowed his head and offered a prayer then and there. God was everywhere, so far as he was concerned, and it didn't matter what anyone else might think. Shortly after I graduated, state accreditation officials forced Brother Rollings to stop teaching school because he lacked proper credentials. Thank God, I got to him before they did!

The Bible: A Daily Guide

Despite mortal errors and limitations to which we all are subject, my parents and teachers performed noteworthy service for which I daily give thanks. One should not suppose that emphasizing memorization meant they regarded the Bible as a mere source of intellectual knowledge. These teachers viewed the Scriptures as a heavenly guide for earthly living.

My parents gave me a copy of the Bible long before I could read it, but more importantly they gave me an example. Mother and Daddy gleaned Scripture's wisdom for daily direction. They consulted its precepts for business decisions. They pleaded its promises in prayer. The Bible framed our lives and inspired our best efforts. Probably not a day passed without someone quoting from Scripture during family conversation. We revered it as the Word of God.

As a child, I was taught not to place any other book or object on top of a Bible. Its ageless words provoked gratitude and humility in our triumphs. It also provided solace in our tragedies and time of grief. How vividly I remember returning to my mother's house after Daddy died in 1972, to find written in large letters on the kitchen chalkboard words from Job, inscribed by my 17-year-old brother Paul:

"The Lord gives and the Lord takes away.
Blessed be the name of the Lord."

Florida College and "Brother Hailey"

After high school, I attended Florida Christian College in Tampa, Florida, which, after my first year, dropped the "Christian" from its name but not from its character. Although it was a junior college, by planning carefully one could attend for three years and graduate the following year from another cooperating school. In 1966, I transferred as a senior to Abilene Christian College.

During my three years at Florida College, I had the extraordinary pleasure of studying under Homer Hailey through 50 semester hours of Bible. Although he already had more than two decades of college teaching under his belt, Brother Hailey always prepared afresh for each class, and he inspired the same diligence in his pupils. Brother Hailey's Bible was "living, active and sharper than any two-edged sword."

This man of God led us verse by verse through all the major and minor prophets of the Old Testament. He was so saturated with their messages that he unconsciously adopted their tone, frequently addressing his own audiences as "my people." We felt the sovereignty of God, the accountability of individuals and nations, and the certainty of judgment. Homer Hailey quoted Amos, Isaiah and Habakkuk in his sermons as freely as most preachers quote from Romans or John or Acts.

When we finished with the prophets, he took us through the Gospel of John, Ephesians, Colossians, Hebrews and the Book of Revelation. If someone then had told me that God later would open doors for me to teach these same lessons in Baptist, Methodist, Presbyterian, Pentecostal, Charismatic, Independent, Advent Christian and Episcopal churches, seminaries and colleges, I could not possibly have believed it.

Brother Hailey required his students to use a hardback edition of the *American Standard Bible*, which contained voluminous references and wide margins for notes. The idea, of course, was to transfer content off the page and into the heart. To this end, one of several requirements for earning an "A" in Brother Hailey's "Scheme of Redemption" course was to memorize Paul's entire epistle to the Ephesians or to the Colossians, then recite it aloud, by appointment, to the professor's secretary. Having preached every Sunday from eleventh grade onward, and wanting to memorize the Scriptures anyway, I earned extra points by reciting both epistles.

Romans Came to Life

After I transferred to Abilene, many truths learned earlier about the basis of our salvation fell into place. Brother Hailey had shown from Leviticus the meaning of sacrificial blood. There a sinful, guilty worshiper brought the substitutionary offering of an animal life—a life which, though amoral, was ceremonially acceptable. We learned from Hebrews how Jesus Christ fulfilled the Old Testament sacrifices, by living in his human body a life of perfect obedience to God, then offering that life to God on the cross in place of ours. But I still did not see clearly how God counts as divinely righteous those who trust in Jesus, or quite understand how that related to me personally.

At Abilene, I continued reading all the Church of Christ periodicals the school library received, as I had previously done at Florida College. As I read the *Gospel Advocate*, which represented the mainline, and the *Gospel Guardian*, an antagonist publication that spoke for the spin-off group in which I had grown up, I was increasingly troubled by the bitter tone and the personal attacks that seemed to fill their respective pages.

"Can this be the purpose of Christ's dying?" I asked myself, and God. "Are the great sagas of Abraham and Moses and Israel supposed to lead to this?" I begged God to show me the true gospel. I solemnly promised that I would teach it and walk it as best I was able for the rest of my life, regardless of public opinion or any other consequences.

As it "happened," my Greek studies that year had us studying and translating the Epistle to the Romans verse by verse. And, before the year was over, the light of that revelation dispelled the shadows in my understanding as it spotlighted the great gospel truth of justification by grace through faith in Jesus Christ—a pronouncement of acquital by God the divine judge which we can never earn, accomplish or deserve, which we can enjoy only as a gift and can access only by trusting faith.

Although I had believed the gospel and had been baptized at age 10, I committed my life anew to Jesus Christ in light of my growing understanding, receiving him by faith as my personal Savior and Lord, claiming his free, divine forgiveness fully wrought at the Cross almost 2,000 years ago. And the more I read Romans, the more irrelevant and unattractive many of the "church papers" became.

New Life with a Beautiful Bride

While at Florida College, I had fallen in love with Sara Faye Locke, a pretty brunette from Franklin, Tennessee, 80 miles up Interstate 65 from my hometown of Athens, Alabama. After our junior college years, Sara Faye transferred to Peabody College in Nashville, later to become a part of Vanderbilt University.

In May of 1967, Sara Faye finished her B.A. degree in English with teacher certification, and I completed my degree in biblical Greek. We married the next month and spent the Summer in Athens, Alabama. I preached for a country church called "Mount Zion," surrounded by other churches with such names as "Ephesus," "Corinth," "New Hope" and "Pleasant Valley."

Sara Faye and I set up housekeeping that Summer in a $65-per-month apartment composed of two small, adjoining motel units. One unit maintained its original form. The bedroom area of the other unit served as combination living/dining room; its tiny bathroom space became a one-person kitchen. Our "furnished" apartment included a red-and-white checkered cafe table and a "Tom's Peanuts" sales case for a china cabinet.

Needless to say, these quarters required a major adjustment for Sara Faye, who had lived her entire life in a neat rock house, which her father had built shortly before he wed. Our neighbors were mostly single and rather boisterous. The first time my in-laws came to visit us, their sleep was interrupted by drunken party-makers diving off our balcony into the swimming pool below.

When August arrived, we loaded our few belongings in a 4x6 U-Haul trailer, hitched it behind my old Chevrolet and hauled it nearly 1,000 miles to Abilene, Texas. The car was not air-conditioned, and Texas in August is H-O-T. "Like getting kicked out of the Garden of Eden," we said, as the rolling hills of Middle Tennessee vanished in our rear-view mirrors. For the next year we woke each morning to view the windy plains of West Texas.

In Abilene, Sara Faye taught eighth grade English while I tried to master Greek in graduate school at Abilene Christian College.

My master's degree program included scriptural and extra-biblical readings in Hebrew and Greek. It climaxed with a thesis which dissected and explained four Pauline passages on Christian unity. While at Abilene Christian, I gained a lifelong love of academic biblical scholarship from teachers such as Tom Olbricht, Everett Ferguson and J. W. Roberts, men who obviously loved God with their minds as well as with their hearts.

Learning from Other Believers

After completing my M.A. in 1968, Sara Faye and I moved to Kirkwood, Missouri, a lovely western suburb of St. Louis, where from 1968-1972, I preached for the local Church of Christ and Sara Faye taught 12th grade English at Kirkwood High School. Driving around the metropolitan area shortly after we arrived, I was quite overwhelmed by the challenge of three million people whom I felt some duty to convert. Later the Lord would graciously show me that I had far more co-workers than I first imagined, and that his eternal, saving program would neither succeed nor fail because of me.

Meanwhile, I enrolled part time at Covenant Theological Seminary and at Eden Theological Seminary nearby, expecting eventually to earn a Ph.D. degree in biblical languages and literature from St. Louis University and move into a teaching career at some seminary or college.

Covenant Seminary was operated by the Reformed Presbyterian Church, Evangelical Synod (now the Presbyterian Church of America). Covenant championed evangelical Christianity, and it provided me the opportunity to enroll in a summer class taught by the late, popular, Christian philosopher and author Francis Schaeffer, who returned to St. Louis from his L'Abri in Switzerland for that purpose.

Eden Seminary belonged to the United Church of Christ (not related to my own variety of Churches of Christ) and represented the liberal Protestant tradition. There I studied under M. Douglas

Meeks, who translated several works of the German theologian Juergen Moltmann, and Lutheran theologian Robert Bertram.

My own church background did not encourage me to consider the faculty or students at either seminary as fully Christian, since they baptized their children while still babies and did so by sprinkling. It was strangely jarring to my mind, therefore, to hear Covenant professors R. Laird Harris and Elmer Smick open class each day with prayer. Not your everyday, garden-variety prayer, mind you, but seasoned prayer that resonated with spiritual depth acquired over years of intimate conversation with the Almighty. I might have expected to hear such prayers from biblical patriarchs or prophets, but not (in my ignorant small-mindedness) from Presbyterians. These men confessed sin, not generically as I had usually heard and done, but thoroughly, from head to toe, exhausting a vocabulary of synonyms for shortcoming and wrongdoing against the Creator of heaven and earth.

Which is easier for God to forgive, I wondered. The person who is baptized "wrong," but who trembles before a holy God and serves him diligently with every fiber of his being? Or the person who is baptized "correctly," lives a moral life and attends church regularly, but whose spiritual thermostat always sits at "mediocre"?

These people at Covenant were serious about God. I decided that I was in no position to judge their relationship with him, regardless of when or how they were baptized. The Scripture seemed to endorse my decision when it said, "The Lord knows those who are his. And let everyone who names the name of Christ depart from iniquity." Later, my joy increased even more as I came better to appreciate that God graciously receives everyone who believes on Jesus Christ as Savior and Lord.

During those years I joined the Society of Biblical Literature and the Evangelical Theological Society, both professional organizations of biblical teachers and scholars. I later published several scholarly articles in the *Journal of the Evangelical Theological*

Society, presented papers at its regional and national meetings, and served one year as a regional vice-president. Through this association I met and befriended contemporary evangelical scholars from many denominations, as well as several men from Churches of Christ who were also venturing into the larger world of evangelical Christianity.

Graduate studies and other scholarly pursuits made me rethink some earlier assumptions as two points became crystal clear. I was impressed, first, with how much all Christians actually share in common—that theological core which C. S. Lewis described as "Mere Christianity." Second, I came to see how believers who are both honest and well-informed can nevertheless reach different conclusions about various spiritual matters.

I also discovered that the intellectual environment can be intoxicating, but God always had a way of bringing me back down to earth. My first scholarly article to be published was titled "The Eschatology of Ignatius of Antioch: Christocentric and Historical." When it appeared, I proudly shared it with my close friend Duane, who served as one of our church elders in Kirkwood. I teased, with a hint of superiority, that he give it to his wife to use in Ladies Bible Class. "I showed your article to Pat," Duane later reported, "but she kept confusing the 'eschatology of Ignatius' with the 'heartbreak of psoriasis.'" Chagrined, I realized how pompous I had been, and remembered the Scripture which warns, "Knowledge puffs up, but love builds up."

Moving into Ministry as God Opened Doors

I had started preaching at rural Alabama churches while in high school, and I regularly filled pulpits for a succession of congregations in Florida and Texas throughout my college years. From 1968 until we moved to Houston in 1982, I served either fulltime or bivocationally as minister for churches in Missouri and Alabama. I usually preached from a larger passage of Scripture rather than choosing a topic and jumping all over the Bible. I explained the historical background of the particular passage, highlighted the meaning of its words and applied its practical principles. Such verse-by-verse teaching was something of a novelty during those years, and audiences seemed to appreciate it wherever I went. I also continued to study the Bible from cover to cover.

While still in high school, I began writing articles for the "church papers" published within our religious circles. By the good graces of numerous editors and the encouragement of their readers, that effort multiplied as years passed. Eventually God opened doors for me to share with much wider audiences through periodicals such as *Moody Monthly* and *Christianity Today*.

While preaching in Kirkwood, Missouri, I wrote a simple Christ-centered gospel booklet entitled *The Grace of God*, which my father published and which was widely used in evangelistic work. Shortly after, I wrote a brief commentary on Romans, then a full-length commentary on Hebrews entitled *Our Man in Heaven*. My friend Gordon asked whom I would pick to write a foreword for the commentary if I could select anyone in the world. Without hesitation, I responded, "F. F. Bruce," a well-known British Bible scholar and commentator who personally belonged to a Brethren church.

"How odd," I thought, "for preachers and teachers in Churches of Christ to read and quote from works by people in other churches, although we could not allow them to teach a class or preach a sermon if they came to our church in person." It also seemed strange that while we regularly depended on the scholarship of others outside our own religious movement, very few people in our heritage had written anything that other people found useful. I determined, with God's help, to write something that could bless believers outside our church fellowship as well as within.

At my friend's urging, I wrote Professor Bruce and asked if he would contribute a foreword to my commentary on Hebrews, which he graciously did—and later a foreword to another book called *The Fire That Consumes* as well. When the first printing of *Our Man in Heaven* had all sold, Baker Book House published a second printing and distributed it to evangelical Christians in general.

During the dozen years from 1970-1982, I penned about 16 books and booklets on biblical topics and texts—a fact I mention only because it illustrates the central place Scripture has occupied throughout my life. I was raised by people of the Book. Other than calling them godly or Christ-like, I can think of no higher compliment one might pay my forebears and mentors than that.

The Scriptures Provide Our Final Standard

From earliest childhood I was taught and still believe that the Scriptures are authoritative, foundational and normative. The Bible is authoritative because it is inspired by the Holy Spirit. In addition, Jesus Christ endorsed the Old Testament Scriptures which, interpreted in light of his life, death and resurrection, resulted in the New Testament Scriptures as well. The Bible is foundational because it is the primary witness to the mighty saving deeds of God culminating in Jesus Christ, and it describes the implications of those deeds for daily living. The Bible is normative because it is the final measure of every other teaching or message that claims divine authority.

That was one important reason why Christians compiled the New Testament books in the earliest centuries of the Church, to serve as a yardstick, or "canon," to measure other teaching said to come from God. It made no difference whether the extra-biblical teaching came through a word of prophecy, a dream or vision, or was passed down from an Apostle or other eyewitness of Jesus. If it contradicted the canon of Scripture, it was wrong— period. If it harmonized with Scripture, it might serve the church, though never on a par with Scripture itself.

But this concept of the Bible as canon is far more than the answer to the question of how the ancient church selected its contents. The canonicity of Scripture is a powerful and practical tool for measuring so-called revelations from God even today, as I was reminded in 1977 when a friend from college days, whom I will call "Ted," passed through our town of Athens, Alabama.

By year's end, Ted warned, Soviet bombs would shower down on America, destroying all but an elect few. He knew this would happen because God had revealed it to a friend of his. Even now, Ted was en route to a pre-ordained survivalist camp somewhere in the Rockies.

My own religious background had not included room for modern-day seers, and I was instinctively skeptical of Ted's apocalyptic message. Lacking any clear scriptural revelation on the topic, I decided to suspend judgment on the oracle until year's end and simply let time pass its verdict. Whatever happened, I would confidently rely on the assurance of the biblical prophet Nahum, that "Jehovah is good, a stronghold in the day of trouble, and he knows those who take refuge in him."

However, the more I learned about Ted, the greater my misgivings grew. More than once, I soon learned, Ted had informed beautiful young women that God wanted them to marry him, strongly suggesting that he could commence carnal relations in the meantime. That was a horse of a different color, since the Bible left no room for doubt on that subject. Such "divine revelation" was simply wrong. Ted might have communicated with some spirit, but it was definitely not the Spirit of God.

I am glad that we have Scripture to use as our measure even today. We may know that, while the Bible's message is not always clear to us, it is always correct. And we can be sure that no authentic communication from God to humans—in any age—ever contradicts the Bible. If any message claiming divine origin disagrees with Scripture it is patently false and we must reject it at once! We join Isaac Watts, passionately and unequivocally, in saying to the Father:

Thy word is everlasting truth.
How pure is every page!
That holy book shall guide our youth,
And well support our age.

As a general rule, we evangelicals do not easily follow false prophets. Instead, our Achille's heel seems to be a tendency to forget that God always transcends his own written word. We should no more imagine that God directs us only through the Scriptures than we would suppose that two spouses who leave each other notes under magnets on the refrigerator door never communicate in any other way.

The Psalmist and Jesus alike would agree with the hymn writer in declaring that "this is my Father's world" and "he speaks to me everywhere." Sometimes God reveals his most intimate messages through the special language of his creation in Nature itself.

TO REFLECT OR DISCUSS

1. Throughout Edward's life, he has always accepted Scripture as the final authority. Yet many of his beliefs have changed over the years. Does that strike you as ironic, or as some thing to be expected?

2. There is a great difference between praising the Bible as God's Word and actually making it a rule of life. How do we move from the first to do the second as well?

3. Has your acquaintance with devout believers from outside your own church circle enlarged your awareness of Christian brotherhood? Is the "fruit of the Spirit" a biblical test for identifying those who belong to Christ?

4. What did Edward discover, as millions before him also had done, to be the heart of the gospel message? Have you made that your own discovery as well?

Chapter 6

The Heavens Declare

In the hush of early morning,
When the breeze is whispering low;
There's a voice that gently calls me,
And its accents well I know.

–Mrs. R. N. Turner

The crisp April air stirred ever so slightly as the sun rose over the Arizona horizon. I shivered in the desert breeze and zipped my light windbreaker a little higher. Two months before, on February 7, 1972, we had sat in freezing rain and watched the undertakers bury Daddy beneath his beloved Alabama soil. He had died suddenly after one week of illness and his death had been a terrible blow. However warm this day might become, a cold numbness still deadened my insides, and a heaviness like lead weighted my aching heart.

I was preacher for the Kirkwood Church of Christ in St. Louis County, Missouri, when Daddy died. Almost a year before, I had committed to this Spring project of preaching every day for three successive weeks in three different congregations in northern Arizona. Sara Faye could not join me because of her work. Since I flew to Arizona and had no car there, I especially appreciated Flagstaff's location in the shadow of the lovely San

Francisco Peaks that first week. The sessions concluded in Cotton-wood, south of scenic Sedona and Oak Creek Canyon. The second week I spent in Winslow, a small town east of Flagstaff.

I had risen early this morning and hiked east out of Winslow, seeking God in the quietness of the desert. Around me, Navajo Indians herded sheep, their reservation sprawling into desert infinity. Dimly visible, three great mesas towered in the distance. Atop these isolated and flat-topped mountains, Hopi Indians dwelt and perpetuated their ancient culture. The barren land-scape extended as far as one could see.

How long had this scene existed? Long before I was born, that was sure, and for hundreds of generations before that. The Bible's opening words came to mind. "In the beginning, God." I knelt there on the desert ground and sang to the Creator. "How great Thou art! How great Thou art!"

In the serenity of these surroundings, I remembered those Bible stories from long ago, and the ancient people who also encountered God in the desert. I thought of Abraham and Moses, Elijah and John the Baptist, and of the Son of God himself. "How insignificant I am," I reflected, "and how short my life at best."

"Yes," the still panorama around me seemed to respond, "but how strong is your Creator, who from everlasting to everlasting is a faithful God." And there, without a word being uttered, in the tranquility of the moment God—as a person—was present. His presence quieted the tumult of my heart. He filled me with joy and hope. He renewed my strength and restored my soul.

Childhood Enriched by God's Creation

Somehow, God has always seemed closer to me when I am out of doors. Even as a child, I was often drawn to step outside at night and simply look at the stars. Since my bed was by a win-dow, I didn't even have to go outside. All I had to do was turn out the lights and moonlight bathed the room. I could lie on my pillow and look up at the heavens, drifting to sleep beneath this twinkling reminder of the eternal One who never sleeps. As far back as I can remember, God communicated through his creation, in hundreds of voices with dozens of accents.

The glorious sunrise heralded each new morning. Trees filled the land of my childhood, and birds filled the trees. Through the day, each sang its special song and not one of them was sad. When evening came, the birds disappeared and the crickets took the stage. Accompanying their serenade were the katydids, the frogs and an unidentified chorale of miscellaneous "bugs." Over it all, the sky glistened with stars so mysteriously distant.

Four distinctive seasons came round in turn, each a welcomed change from the one before, staying just long enough to create a desire for the next. Few pleasures in life compare with the experience of a Summer rain shower when you are about ten years old. You could feel it in the air and smell it coming on the wind! The freshness of that aroma is stored indelibly in my mind to this day. The whole universe told me that God is unspeakably powerful. I agreed with Genesis: it was "very good." And I was blissfully happy.

The English word "poem" comes from a Greek word that refers, among other things, to an artist's composition or a craftsman's handiwork. The Apostle Paul uses the word twice of God's workmanship, once of the physical creation, and once of the believer's life of good works. Paul would agree with David who wrote that "the heavens declare the glory of God, and the firmament shows his handiwork."

Our formal worship also acknowledges God s message communicated through nature. "This is my Father's world," the hymn declares, "and to my listening ears all nature sings, and round me rings the music of the spheres." The original sin of most human beings, according to the Apostle Paul in Romans, is to ignore God's message proclaimed in creation itself. God reveals himself so powerfully in nature that every rational person on earth can "get the message"—that there is a God who made all this, to whom our proper response as creatures is humility and gratitude at the least. There is no excuse for ignoring this message, the Apostle says, even if one has never seen a Bible or heard a sermon and cannot read or write. God has made himself known to all through his creation.

The Fudges didn't take many vacations when I was growing up. Daddy's notion of resting was to work for a while at a different task. The few vacations I do remember were camping trips to the Smoky Mountains, and what a cache of memories those outings deposited! God spoke to me in the song of the mountain streams, the whisper of the cool breeze, the constant background of the forest creatures praising their Creator without guile. "Unto the Hills" became one of my favorite psalms and favorite hymns as a result of such trips.

From ages 13-17, I spent two weeks each summer at Camp Wyldewood, a Christian camp near Searcy, Arkansas. Wyldewood was coeducational, with girls' cabins lining off one side of the main area and a row of boys' cabins marking off the other. The entire grounds were heavily wooded. At the outskirts rose a rocky bluff and at its base flowed the Little Red River. We had devotionals in the open air, or under roofed structures without walls. The woods were our cathedrals. If there had not been mosquitoes to remind us otherwise, we might have imagined we were in Paradise.

My fascination with nature's charms spiraled during my final two years at Athens Bible School, when I studied American and English Literature under Brother Rollings. He did not teach literature in the conventional manner of critical analysis, but simply read poetry for its own sheer majesty and beauty. He invited us to follow him into a magical world of nature unmarred by sin, a secret place where birds and flowers and trees came alive, eager to share the mysteries of an unbroken communion with God.

In that utopian world, Bryant's waterfowl testified to God's unerring providence, to which Shelley's skylark responded in quiet trust. Emerson's rhodora assured us that God is praised by being, as well as by doing, and Holmes' chambered nautilus challenged us to become all that our created potential allowed. Thomas Gray may have written his "Elegy" in a church graveyard, but it eloquently portrayed the possibilities and grandeur of life on God's earth, however simple and obscure that life might be.

Inner Strength During Desolate Times

The Arizona meetings ended and I returned to St. Louis to wind up affairs for our move back to Athens, Alabama, to help Mother with the family publishing business. The details are part of another chapter, but from 1972 to 1975, I watched every earthly security vanish before my eyes, beginning with my father, the family business, my job, and then my own reputation.

It appeared that God had forgotten me. At times I wondered if he could ever find me, even if he looked. But even the darkness of those circumstances could not block God's encouraging voice, as he consoled me almost daily through the world he had made. And later, when the light dawned again, I came to understand that God had temporarily extinguished my hope in earthly things to strengthen my faith in the One who is eternal.

By 1976, I was working as a typesetter in a commercial print shop in Decatur, Alabama, 14 miles south of Athens on the banks of the Tennessee River. The job was sedentary and I needed exercise, so I decided to spend my lunch hour walking. Most days I trekked with an apple in one hand and a devotional book in the other, meanwhile talking to the Lord.

Decatur is a grand old town in the best Southern tradition. It boasts some elegant residential streets, canopied by giant oak trees planted on either side with tops that meet in the middle. Few people ventured out during lunch hour, though even in Summer I found the weather fairly pleasant in the shade. Some days I walked to the river and stood on its banks, or sat on a huge concrete support under the bridge.

During the six years I worked at the print shop, I learned to trust God in a new and deeper way—first his love, then his wisdom and finally his timing. Scripture verses I had memorized years before concerning God's care and providence acquired new meaning in the cauldron of personal uncertainty and fear. The beautiful creation around me served as God's silent arms, embracing me and holding me close even while my questions of "Why?" and "When?" went unanswered.

Supported by these surroundings, I learned to surrender my own dreams and ambitions to God. With that surrender came an intimacy with God that more than compensated for all I had lost, and a bedrock assurance of God's faithfulness—a confidence that provided a foundation for the rest of my life.

God answered my earlier requests for his guidance but he also gave me something far greater—the experiential knowledge of God himself as the living, personal God who sees us, hears us, and who sometimes answers our prayers in immediate and dramatic ways. That is exactly what happened the night I prayed desperately for my younger brother Benjamin, who was separated from me by more than 3,000 miles.

Above the Stars, God Really Hears!

A young, single man, Benji had moved to the Northwest, away from home and, for a time, away from God. But God followed him there and eventually he brought Benji back to Athens and back to himself. At last, Benji had decided to return to the Northwest. He said he needed to prove to himself the genuineness of God's work and presence in his own life. With tears and much prayer, we said goodbye and he moved from the lower right side of the U.S. map to its top left side.

Although we normally maintained close contact, I had not heard from my brother for several weeks, and I was beginning to feel some concern. He lived in a remote place, away from any town, and there was reason to fear for his physical and spiritual safety alike. As the days passed, my anxiety continued to increase.

About 9:00 o'clock one evening, I felt a special burden for Benji's welfare and went into my own backyard to pray. It was a wonderful place for prayer, bordered by trees on either side, with a large pasture behind. My house provided privacy in front. No one could see me kneeling there but God, looking down, as I imagined, through a million stars overhead.

"Please, Lord," I begged, "take care of Benjamin. He is trusting in you, and I know you are faithful." Many times in life we simply do not know how to pray, or what to pray for. This was such a time. Circumstances called for a daring request; God could respond as he saw fit.

"You are almighty," I said, "and you know exactly where Benji is this very minute, although I do not. Would you please make yourself known to him right now? And, if you would be so kind, please let me know somehow that he is okay as well." This prayer was born of necessity, not learned at church.

Certain that God had heard my plea and content that he would do whatever was best. I rose from the ground and began walking back toward the house. I was probably 20 feet from the door when it opened and Sara Faye called out. "It's the phone... for you," she said. "I think it's Benji."

I rushed inside, my heart overflowing with emotion. "Hello," said the familiar voice on the other end of the line. "This is Benjamin, and something very strange just happened. I was about to go out for the evening and had already put on my coat. In fact, I was at the door, when suddenly I had this overwhelming feeling that I was supposed to call you. So I did. Is anything wrong?"

"No, everything is RIGHT!" I said. Then, with tears of gratitude streaming down my cheeks, I told my brother how God had just heard a prayer from a backyard in Alabama and had graciously and immediately answered it by a telephone call from

Oregon, more than 3,000 miles away. Never again would I wonder whether God could see any of his children, no matter where
they might be.

TO REFLECT OR DISCUSS

1. Has nature ever been God's "voice" to you? Think about the
   circumstances when that was true, and recall the effect of this
   "voice" in your own life.

2. Identify some biblical characters whose lives involved the outdoors. How did their natural environments shape or match the
   spirituality, for example, of David, Elijah, John the Baptist and
   even Jesus?

3. Have you ever received a dramatic answer to prayer, such as
   Edward's call from his brother Benjamin? What did you feel
   in response? If that has not been your experience yet, what
   do you think your response would be if it occurred?

Chapter 7

The Spirit's Sword

More about Jesus let me learn,
More of his holy will discern;
Spirit of God, my teacher be,
Showing the things of Christ to me.

–E. E. Hewitt

"I need your understanding and help," I told Sara Faye one Summer morning in 1977, feeling somewhat embarrassed and frankly confused. "I don't quite know how to say this, but I've got to do something today that I've never done before. The only thing I can compare it to is Jacob's wrestling with the angel."

My wife had encountered many surprises during our eleven years of marriage, and she had usually coped with marvelous grace, but this was another first. She knew that I had struggled since college days with several thorny doctrinal problems. One concerned salvation and baptism; another involved spiritual gifts. "Can someone be saved who has not been properly baptized by immersion?" I still asked, even after my recent experiences at Covenant Seminary. "And what about spiritual gifts today—especially those unusual ones such as tongues, prophecy and healing? Does God still give these gifts, or were they only for an ancient era?"

My own background had provided answers on both topics, to be sure. Dogmatic answers that left no possible room for doubt or even further discussion. No one is saved without being immersed in water, we said, and salvation comes not a moment before. Spiritual gifts of the "miraculous" variety, such as tongues and healing and prophecy, merely "filled in" until the New Testament was written, and then they ceased. That was what we said. Period.

These answers were firm and clear. Perhaps too firm and clear, I thought. Indeed, the more I studied the Bible and church history, and the more believers I encountered and came to know outside our own religious fellowship, the less my long-held answers seemed to satisfy. Rather than subsiding, the inner struggle intensified with the passing of time, stimulated both by careful Bible study and by wider acquaintances with Christians of backgrounds other than my own. When I woke on this particular day, I sensed that the time had arrived for conclusions.

The Verse that Seemed to Jump off the Page

"So," I said to my wife, who had long since quit trying to understand her husband's eccentricities, "I've got to go to a quiet and private place where I can be alone and undisturbed. I'm going to fast and pray today until some answers come. From what I read in the Bible, fasting shows God how serious and even desperate someone is in seeking his will. That is all I desire, and I know God wants us to know that."

"How do you expect to get an answer?"

"I don't have the slightest idea," I said. "Any way God sees fit to reveal it—through the Bible, by sending someone to talk to me, by a word from heaven, or by an inner understanding. That is up to him. But I have to find some answers. Please pray for me as the day progresses."

"I'll do that," she assured, "and I hope you find whatever you're looking for.

So, taking my well-worn Bible and a heavy but hopeful heart, I drove 20 miles out of town to an isolated and heavily wooded park, determined not to eat or return home until God provided answers and calmed the intellectual storms that raged inside my head. Pulling off the road into the trees, I parked the car, put my Bible on a concrete picnic table, and walked into the forest. Overhead, leaves rustled in the morning breeze and the birds sang all around.

"Father," I began, "you say in your Word that you lead us in paths of righteousness for your name's sake. I beg you to reveal your ways to me on these matters today. This is more important to me than food or drink. I must know your will about the relation between salvation and baptism—and about spiritual gifts. I have no agenda of my own. I do not care what any other person says or thinks. All I want is your will. If you will reveal it to me, I will stand by it, teach it, preach it and be faithful to it—no matter what the consequences."

I prayed and prayed, in every way I knew or could imagine. I prayed walking, kneeling and lying on the ground. I cried out with a loud voice and pleaded softly, sobbing. I quoted Scripture to God, surrendering my heart and mind and will, seeking only to understand his Word.

After an hour or two, I returned to the concrete picnic table and picked up the Bible. God had not sent any messenger my way, whether human, animal or angel. He had not spoken to me, audibly or in my heart. Perhaps he would answer me through his written Word. "Please speak to me, Lord, and I will listen," I pleaded and promised. "Lead me to some Scripture, if you will, that answers my questions."

I had heard preachers criticize people who sought guidance by letting their Bibles fall open at random, then pointing to the page with their eyes closed. A most unreliable method, as a general rule. But this was not an ordinary situation. I was desperate. Anyway, that approach was certainly no stranger than Gideon putting out fleece, or the high priest in the Old Testament reaching into a pouch for Urim and Thummim stones, or disciples in the New Testament making decisions by casting lots.

"Doesn't God control this material universe?" I asked myself. "Couldn't the sovereign Lord who once made a river flow upstream, turned a sun dial backwards and made city walls fall, also regulate the force of gravity on one man's copy of the Scriptures if he so willed?"

I stood my Bible on its spine, said another prayer and turned it loose. It opened to the Psalms—about midway through. Nothing strange about that. Center of gravity. I began reading.

I do not know how long I had read before it happened. "A revelation," some people call it. An "encounter with God." I cannot name the experience that occurred next. I can only describe it, and say that God emblazoned it into my heart and soul from that day to this. As I was reading Psalm 115, my eyes came upon verse three. Suddenly it was as if the words jumped off the page and hit me squarely between the eyes. I did not hear any audible voice, but the confidence that God spoke to me could not have been more certain if I had. The words crashed into my consciousness like a thunderbolt: "Our God is in the heavens, and he does whatever he pleases."

Immediately I knew that this was God's answer to both my struggles. Who is saved? Whomever God wishes to save! What about spiritual gifts? God does whatever he pleases! He is GOD. We are not. That message became even clearer later. But this was enough for now. "Thank you, God!" I exclaimed. "Thank you, thank you, thank you!"

With that, I turned to the New Testament Gospel of John, because it says that it is written for the express purpose of creating faith and bringing salvation. I began highlighting every saying of Jesus concerning the believer:

Whoever believes in the Son has life.
The believer is not condemned.

No one can snatch the believer out of the Father's hands.

God has given believers to Jesus and he will not lose any of them but raise them up in the last day.

"These are your words, Lord Jesus," I said, marking these statements of Jesus and many others like them. "I know they are true and that I can depend on them. I promise to say them, without fear or compromise, as long as I live. If, on the Day of Judgment, I am called to account for saying these words—and I mean this respectfully—I will point to You and say that You told me these things."

When I finished reading John's Gospel, I turned to the First Epistle of John, because this letter says it is written so we may know that we have eternal life. As I read, an incredible peace flooded over my soul and I silently wept for joy. I was not trying to prove anything; I only desired to know the will of God.

Faith and Baptism Go Together

Next I turned to the Acts of the Apostles, the book from which I had heard so many sermons as a child. The book so full of baptisms. The book that contained so many of our favorite verses on that subject. I resolved to be true to this New Testament book as well. Whatever it said, I determined to say—under the same or similar circumstances. As I read John's Gospel and Acts side by side, I was impressed with a wonderful thought. There is a time and place for all of this, I realized. Christians have fought and debated because someone lost the proper balance, often on both sides.

If one asks the basis on which we receive salvation, the Gospel of John answers clearly. It is by trusting in Christ—nothing more, nothing less and nothing else. But if one says he or she does trust Christ and asks what to do next, the Book of Acts answers with equal clarity. Be baptized promptly in Jesus' name, publicly expressing by this act of obedience the faith that is deep inside the heart. I do not have to know how all this works. I just have to state both truths, each in its proper turn. "Our God is in the heavens, and he does whatever he pleases!"

God Sovereignly Bestows Spiritual Gifts

Time flew now as I eagerly searched the Scriptures—passages I had read in English and Greek for many years—texts I had memorized in high school or even learned as a child. I turned to First Corinthians and eagerly devoured everything it said about spiritual gifts. Then I read from Ephesians, and from First Peter. At last, for me, the inspired writings fell into place. Many others had discovered these truths long before I had. Now God was graciously confirming and impressing them on me as well.

One person receives one gift, another something different. "Our God is in the heavens, and he does whatever he pleases!" Some people see miracles while others do not. "Our God is in the heavens, and he does whatever he pleases!" Church history records an abundance of extraordinary gifts at certain times in various countries, but not in other periods or places. "Our God is in the heavens, and he does whatever he pleases!"

"Dear heavenly Father," I prayed, "please give me whatever gifts will honor and glorify you, and every gift you wish to give me to bless others. I want everything you consent to give, and I will be content with your decision. You are God. You are in the heavens. Please do whatever you please!"

During the following days and weeks God was apparently pleased to give me extraordinary peace and joy—frequently in waves of heavenly happiness which made me laugh out loud for sheer delight. "What's wrong with you, fool?" a fellow-worker sometimes asked when that happened, and I always told him it was God's wonderful Spirit.

Indeed, John's Gospel promises God's "fullness" which he pours out upon us, "grace upon grace." Jesus promised believers the abiding Holy Spirit, who, like an artesian well deep inside our souls, gushes to the surface and overflows in eternal life. Paul once describes the Kingdom of God as "righteousness, joy and peace in the Holy Spirit." God's gifts are varied and many, but the greatest gift is the Giver himself. T. O. Chisholm expressed it so well in the hymn that says:

> "Be with me. Lord! No other gift or blessing
> Thou couldst bestow could with this one compare—
> A constant sense of Thy abiding presence,
> Where'er I am, to feel that Thou art near."

The Spirit's "Sword" Has a Sharp Point

This was not the first or last time God's Spirit spoke to me through the written Scriptures. Often the Spirit does so to convict me of sin. How well I remember the first time that occurred to me, as a boy in eighth grade. Several buddies and I had decided to go camping in the country overnight. One of the boys had an older brother who acted as our driver.

My father knew that some of these boys smoked tobacco and drank beer, both practices forbidden to me. When I telephoned his office to ask about going, he warned me mildly. "Be careful," he said. "You are going with some boys who do some things that you are not supposed to do!"

My Dad did not know it, but I had previously acquired a corn-cob pipe as a souvenir and had already stuck it in my bag of camping supplies, intending to buy some smoking tobacco on the way to our destination. Before leaving the house, I happened to pick up my *King James Bible* and "accidentally" opened it to Romans chapter 13. What should my eyes fall on but the verse that said, "put ye on the Lord Jesus Christ, and make no provision for the flesh, to fulfill the lusts thereof." I squirmed as I read these words, especially the command: "make no provision." I was caught in the very act.

I did not yet know the marvelous story of Saint Augustine's conversion, and how this same passage spoke to him. Certainly my circumstances as a church-going child differed greatly from his as a profligate grown man. But we had this much in common at least. We both learned that while this book called the Bible could be memorized, it could not be managed. A divine force was loose in it, a spiritual energy that could slice right through external appearances and pretensions of piety, directly to the core of one's being. This was indeed the "sword of the Spirit."

The Comfort of the Scriptures

The Holy Spirit also mightily used God's written Word to comfort me immediately after Daddy died in 1972. Anyone who has lost a parent, or other close relative or dear friend, knows the inexpressible emptiness, the heaviness in the pit of the stomach, the sense of fatigue and hopelessness that grief can generate, an insatiable gnawing that can consume you like a beast of prey.

Daddy died in February, and Sara Faye and I moved back to Athens in late August. During the months following the move, I often read the Bible specifically for consolation, looking for a word of hope, asking God to comfort me. One day, God spoke to me powerfully through a passage in the Psalms. "God is a father to the fatherless," the text said. It was as if the passage had my name in it. I claimed the promise with confidence and pleaded it with persistence.

"My Daddy has died," I told God. "I have no earthly father any more. You must be my father now in a special way." As always, God was faithful to his Word. Over the next few years, he comforted and restored my soul. The words on the page of the Bible came alive in my moment of need as the Holy Spirit used the written Word, his spiritual sword.

There were other, more tangible, needs as well, to which the Spirit spoke through the written Word. When we returned to Athens after Daddy's death in 1972, our living standard took a nosedive. In Kirkwood, we had enjoyed my preaching salary from the church plus Sara Faye's wages as a teacher. In addition, we had no house payment because we lived in the church parsonage. And we had no children.

In Athens, I earned $80 per week salary in the family publishing business. We moved there in the middle of a week, and before Sunday a congregation in the county had offered me a job as their weekly preacher. The church said it could pay me $80 per week, and later raised that to $100.

Sara Faye was pregnant with Melanie, our first child, and she chose not to work outside the home until our children reached school age. We built a new house—and assumed monthly payments. Even though our mortgage payment was barely over $200 each month, that amount was still a hefty sum in relation to my total income. In 1975, when Melanie was 2 1/2 years old, Jeremy was born and that made four of us.

The years from 1972-1975 brought many radical changes in our lives. After Daddy died, Mother sold the family publishing business to a consortium of businessmen who belonged to our particular wing of the Churches of Christ. However, she continued to manage the business and I was in charge of editing and production. My own emphasis on God's grace and the necessity of trusting Christ alone for salvation, rather than church membership, correct doctrine or our own obedience, had sparked rumblings of dissent for several years from some within our narrow religious segment.

Now I was at CEI, the publishing business my parents had built from scratch so long before. Although we primarily published books, my father had also acquired a religious periodical called the *Gospel Guardian* shortly before he died. The publication had a contentious history, but Daddy hoped to reform it for more constructive purposes.

However, my religious opponents regarded this new involvement with CEI and the *Guardian* as dangerously influential. They therefore launched a sustained public attack on my teaching, through another journal that they controlled, and which they used quite successfully to control their own scattered constituency.

These adversaries also invaded my home county as two of their scrappiest debaters traveled to several Limestone County churches to denounce me personally by name. As a visual aid, they displayed a full-size bed sheet on which they had drawn a large sailing vessel connected to many anchors. However, all the ropes securing the anchors were cut with little axes. In block letters across the top of the sheet a caption proclaimed:

"THE FALSE TEACHINGS OF ED FUDGE HAVE CHOPPED THE ANCHORS THAT HOLD THE SHIP OF ZION!"

Through such means, these persistent foes sowed suspicion and distrust among many of my lifelong friends, and their intimidating tactics closed numerous pulpits to me which were previously open. (Besides all that, my name is Edward and I have never liked to be called Ed.) All this they did in the name of God, whom I am sure they thought they were serving.

Early in the summer of 1975, after three years of frequent sniping, my opponents culminated a secret purchase of our family business from the group of men who originally bought it from Mother. Our owners told us only that there was a new buyer. We did not learn his identity until he arrived at our offices that hot day in July. As it happened, the new owner was a wealthy West Coast entrepreneur who largely sponsored the enterprise that had been attacking me and others who advocated the gospel of grace. Also accompanying him to our offices in Athens, Alabama were his two "advisors"—the publisher and editor of the opposition magazine!

The publisher, a veteran religious debater of considerable personal force, called me into my mother's office for a tete-a-tete. He asked if I still held certain views I had previously published in my little booklet entitled *The Grace of God*. I confirmed that I did. "I am sorry you hold those teachings," he said. "If you should ever see the light and teach the truth, Brother So-and-So (the new owner of our business) is a very generous man and I believe he would make sure your family was provided for."

I told him unequivocally that my convictions were not for sale. Then, paraphrasing Peter's comment to Simon the Sorcerer—"Your money perish with you!"—I suggested that his benefactor could take his money and go to hell. At that, the publisher's expression hardened and he abruptly left the room. Soon our chief corporate officer, who now worked for the new owner, came into the room. There, in my mother's office, under my father's portrait, he informed me that I was fired from the family business.

With that news and three weeks' pay in my pocket, I went home to my wife, our daughter Melanie, age two-and-a-half, and son Jeremy, barely two weeks old. Although I scurried and scrambled and tried several methods of self-employment, for the next 18 months my regular earnings consisted of $100.00 per week from the country church where I had preached since moving to Athens in 1972.

God Always Keeps His Promises

In these circumstances, Sara Faye and I learned to pray for daily needs as never before. Not as a religious exercise, or to fulfill a spiritual duty. We prayed to survive! We had no savings, no regular job, no earthly sponsor or mentor—no one else to depend on but God. How often we turned to Jesus' words in the Sermon on the Mount, where the Lord pointed to the birds and flowers and urged us to trust God to care for us as well as for them. We clung to this promise and others like it.

Very often, at the beginning of a new month I held up the bills in one hand and my meager income in the other and discussed the situation with the Lord. "Father," I would say, "you see these bills and you see this money, and you see that the bills are greater than the money. Jesus said that if we seek your kingdom first, you will supply our daily needs. I need you to do that for me now, Lord."

In this way we put God to his Word, time after time, and he was always faithful. Many times we went to the mailbox to find a check from someone in a distant state whom we had not seen or heard from in years. "We just happened to think of you," a letter would say, "and wondered how you are doing. God has blessed us and we wanted to share this with you." Inside we would find a check—usually just enough to meet essential needs until the next time around.

Shortly after they snatched our family business, the antagonists boasted in their magazine that, although they had not completely destroyed my influence, they had succeeded in driving me underground. However, they failed to reckon with the fact that Jesus holds the keys to human history and that he can open doors that no mortal can close. In fact, their very opposition set the stage for God to fulfill that promise in a mighty way.

These adversaries destroyed my reputation within the scope of their shrinking sectarian brotherhood. However, during the coming years God honored me with the respect and encouragement of faithful brothers and sisters in the broader fellowship of Churches of Christ and far across the larger Christian spectrum. These foes effectively closed pulpits to me in places they exercised influence, but God opened doors for me to minister in classrooms, pulpits and publications reaching literally around the world.

The darkness of my circumstances drove me again and again to the light of God's Word. I made the hymn words my frequent prayer: "Spirit of God, my teacher be; showing the things of Christ to me." Time after time, precious promises of the Bible spoke with power as the Holy Spirit applied them to my heart. These were not merely words on a page, nor even words from a holy book. They were living words. They were spirit and life. They were God's words—to me personally.

And, while he never contradicts anything in his written Word, God could speak in other ways, too, as I was also about to learn.

TO REFLECT OR DISCUSS

1. How has God spoken directly to your heart through a particular passage of Scripture?

2. Why do you think God sometimes allows all earthly securities to vanish in the lives of those who are devoted to him?

3. Have you ever "put God to his word" by claiming a specific scriptural promise, and then seen God keep that promise? How is that different from testing God in a forbidden sense?

4. How do we move from religiosity (head knowledge and church attendance) to a daily, personal relationship with the Living God? What part does adversity sometimes have in that process?

Chapter 8

A Still, Small Voice

He speaks, and the sound of his voice
Is so sweet the birds hush their singing;
And the melody that He gave to me,
Within my heart is ringing.

–C. Austin Miles

Within days after I was fired from the publishing company in July 1975, an idea came to me for another business to help put bread on the table. "Personalized Publishing Services" sprang from the fact that most people who write manuscripts cannot find a publisher who is willing to assume the financial risk required to produce a book.

Many of these unpublished authors simply stash their manuscripts and hope for a better day. Others decide to publish their own works. However, the cost of a commercial printer is often prohibitive, and most writers lack the technical knowledge and expertise needed to select typefaces, design and lay out pages, illustrate a cover, register a copyright, and make all the other decisions involved in publishing a book.

God Graciously Provided "Manna"

My plan was to offer such authors a complete menu of services commencing with their manuscript and concluding with a finished book. If they wished, I could even introduce their book to several hundred Christian booksellers via a printed brochure. I charged actual costs plus a mark-up for my services but, because of my previous experience and contacts, could often still offer a price less than the author could find for printing alone.

This concept came to me so fast and fluently that I literally sat down at a typewriter one evening and, within an hour, hammered out a two-page brochure in question-answer form that explained my services. I mailed a handful of the brochures to a half-dozen Christian publishers I knew quite well, and requested that they enclose one with their rejection letter to authors whose manuscripts they decided not to publish.

About three weeks later, a Christian Church minister in a midwestern state telephoned to say that he had a manuscript, complete with numerous full-color photographs, that he hoped to distribute in book form at a conference to be held in about 90 days. With the help of a "Mom and Pop" printer nearby, I produced his book in record time, charging enough to earn $100 per week profit for my efforts. Just as that job was completed another one came. So God provided, with manna-like regularity and steadfastness, for the next year and a half.

For many years my father had maintained a close relationship with a printer in Decatur, Alabama, 14 miles down the road from Athens, so much so that the Decatur Printing Company premises had become as familiar to me as our own offices. After I left the family business, I continued to patronize this same shop for much of my own printing.

One day in 1976, I went to Decatur Printing Company to get a price quotation and happened to encounter one of the two owners. He had just bought a new electronic typesetting machine, he said, and he was looking for somebody to operate it. I told him that I needed a job and was willing to learn the machine if he was interested. He offered me the job and I started work the next week, earning $7.00 an hour. That was the best-paying job I had held to that time, and I was exceedingly grateful to find it.

Curiously, when I started working at Decatur Printing Company, the flow of manuscripts to Personalized Publishing Services stopped—almost to the very day. Like the manna which ended at the Promised Land, God timed his faithful provision precisely according to the need. Some people can apparently manage an excess of provisions and God blesses them with abundance. He has usually taken care of me on a week-to-week basis, regardless of the size of my paycheck. Perhaps he knows that I need to be reminded constantly of my complete dependence on him.

I Knew I Was Nailed

The owners at Decatur Printing Company were very good to me, and I gave thanks every day for them and for my job. After a year or two, however, I also found myself praying every day for God to deliver me from the typesetting job. I had a graduate degree in biblical languages and a decade of work experience, first as a minister then as an editor and publisher. I became almost obsessed with the thought that I should have a job more in keeping with my gifts and training. Many days I told the Lord about this problem while driving to work in the morning, during my lunch hour, and again while returning home.

One morning going to work I was feeling particularly sorry for myself, and just a little angry at God. "What's going on, anyway?" I asked the Almighty. "You gave me natural gifts of oral communication and writing. You permitted me to obtain a good education, including a master's degree and additional work at seminary. You have led me into experiences in several fields and given me countless contacts in varied areas of Christian ministry. Yet here I am—stuck at this print shop in a remote corner of Alabama where nobody even knows I exist. Where has all this gotten me, anyway?"

Before my words died in the air, it seemed that God answered. Not aloud, but in words nevertheless, two electrifying and straightforward sentences that bypassed my ears and communicated directly to my brain. "You've got the question wrong," I distinctly heard inside my head. "It's not where has this gotten you, but have you been faithful with what you have been given?"

Like Job of old, I knew when I was nailed. "Of course that is the question. Lord," I replied. "I was selfish and wrong. You are God and I am your servant. And I have tried very hard to be faithful with what you have given me."

Can I prove it was God who spoke to my mind that day? I cannot, of course. Am I convinced it was the Lord? I am, without a doubt. The message was in agreement with Scripture. It convicted me of my own pride and self-centeredness. It redirected me to the correct focal point in life—of faithfulness to God and service to his glory. This was the first time I had "heard" God in such a direct manner, but it was not the last. The next time he condescended to speak to me, it was out of love for my wife, whom I did not have sense enough to cherish and care for as I ought.

Discovering the God who Changes Lives

The last week in September of 1975, Sara Faye and I drove to Massachusetts where I preached for a week at an extraordinary church in the Boston suburb of Wakefield. Those seven days changed our lives forever. The Wakefield Church of Christ began from the evangelistic outreach of a layman named Bob, a supervisor at an electronics plant and an avid body builder.

Bob had met Christ through a door-to-door missionary. He excitedly shared the good news, first with his own eight children, then with their friends. Soon he began a Bible study at his house. When it outgrew the room, he knocked out a wall to accommodate even more people. Within four years, Bob personally led more than 300 young people to faith in Christ and baptized them with his own hands.

At first, these new converts visited a church in a nearby town, usually hitchhiking or riding bikes. The host church tried to be hospitable, but these new converts, unaccustomed to churchly etiquette, just didn't fit in. Soon they started a church in their own town of Wakefield, meeting on Sunday mornings in a rented school auditorium. When we arrived there that September, the Wakefield Church numbered about 200.

This was a congregation like none I had ever seen. It included former alcoholics, drug addicts and prostitutes. I met one new believer, a distinguished, white-haired gentleman, who had reigned over a pornography racket in the Boston area before he met Jesus Christ. Mike, who taught a Sunday evening Bible study, had heard the gospel while in jail for armed robbery.

Then there was Skippy. Skippy was a Satan-worshipper when he first heard about Bob's home Bible class. He decided to visit the class, half out of curiosity and half to cause trouble. But Skippy's reputation preceded him. The first time he attended, Skippy sat on the floor in a corner near Bob. "Glad to have you here, Skippy," Bob said. "They tell me you worship the devil."

"That's right," Skippy replied.

"They tell me you can go into a trance whenever you want to."

"That's right."

"Skippy," the muscular man standing over him asked, "do you see this fist? The first time I see your eyes shut during my Bible class, I'm going to put you into a trance that you won't come out of for a week!"

Needless to say, Skippy didn't go into a trance, and eventually he committed his life to Christ and was baptized. I had the pleasure of talking to him after the service on Sunday morning. "I had three choices," he told me. "I could either be dead, or in jail, or become a Christian. I decided to be a Christian."

Although I grew up in the heart of the Bible Belt, I had never witnessed a radical conversion from open ungodliness. In fact, at the time I did not know anyone who had been saved directly from the world. My fellow church members back home had either been born into a Christian family or had switched to our church from some other Christian group.

Most of the believers in Wakefield had no experience in "doing church," so they did whatever came naturally. Many of the boys had long hair, which then would have excluded them automatically from most churches of my acquaintance. Some people wandered around during the service that Sunday morning. Others, without intending any disrespect, smoked inside the building.

Their theology came straight from the Bible, which they took at face value. Their worship was vibrant and uninhibited. They used regular hymnals, but they also sang many Scripture choruses and contemporary praise songs that I had never heard. Their praise and thanksgiving bubbled over from deep inside. They prayed about specific, actual needs—and they sounded like they expected God to provide in tangible ways.

When time came for communion, one of the servers picked up the bread to pray. "But first," he said, "I have an announcement. Today I am one year old (in the Lord)!" Everyone applauded. Then he bowed his head and thanked God for saving us, and for the Lord's Supper, which commemorates that great salvation.

I felt as if I were seeing the Book of Acts come alive. Later, as we returned to Alabama, Sara Faye and I wondered whether we could experience that same vitality and freshness back at home. We had seen an obvious work of God, and we were certain that only God could perform it. Equally clearly, he could work whenever and wherever he desired. We determined to seek God, then wait and see what he might do.

Seeking God Back in Alabama

When we returned home, we shared these experiences with several friends who also expressed a desire for power and renewal in their own spiritual lives. We decided to open our home on Tuesday nights to anyone who desired to come for a period of praise, Bible reading and prayer. Our group fluctuated from week to week, and it included a genuine cross-section of individuals. We were black and white, prosperous and poor, men and women, young and old.

After a period of singing praises, we typically read a short New Testament book straight through without comment, then discussed its implications for our lives. We concluded with a season of prayer, open to anyone who wished to participate. It was the first time some of the women had ever prayed aloud in public, and the first time some of the men had ever heard a woman pray. Over the next year, the Tuesday night meetings provided such blessing, and the bond between us grew so strong and sweet, that the little group decided to form a new church.

During that same year, the country church for which I had been preaching decided to terminate our relationship. They had never had a preacher for more than two years, they told me, and I had been there for four. They also said that they were not accusing me of saying it outright, but some of the members had surmised that I thought the Methodists and Baptists might also go to heaven. I had also stirred up a small tempest one evening during a recent revival when I invited a visiting black brother to lead the opening prayer.

We interpreted that development as a sign of God's guidance. Soon our Tuesday night group started meeting on Sundays in a shopping center. Our little sign over the door announced, "A Meeting Place for Christians." After several months, we moved to a renovated barn that had been a veterinarian's clinic, and added another line to our sign which now said, "Elm Street Church: A Meeting Place for Christians."

Although we encountered occasional problems common to sinful human beings, the Elm Street experience was overwhelmingly positive. Since we started from ground zero, we enjoyed developing our own traditions and style, in a county with nearly as many churches as rocks, and where most churches viewed any originality as only a notch or two short of the original sin. We loved each other like family, and the fellowship was rich and warm.

Worship meetings focused on Jesus, included far more praise than petition, and, though actually spontaneous, seemed always to follow a timely theme. In this setting, old hymns took on fresh meaning, and familiar passages of Scripture often gleamed with new light as we attempted to center our thinking on Jesus and the core gospel. From the beginning, we chose intimacy with God and holiness of life as our priorities, consciously deciding to let numerical growth take care of itself.

Since we had no paid staff, the financial offerings of two Sundays more than covered our expenses; the remainder of our offerings we spent for gospel outreach or gave to the poor. Our nonsectarian, nondenominational approach confused many of our neighbors, who had not seen Christianity in that form before. One of our brothers once took a truckload of coal to a poor family in need of fuel, explaining that it was a gift from some believers with whom he worshiped.

"What denomination?" the recipient asked, with natural curiosity.

"No denomination," the brother said. "Just a group of Christians."

The man persisted in asking the identity of this strange church. Frustrated with what he considered unnecessary details, our benevolent brother finally replied, "Just say Jesus sent it, and he's sorry he couldn't send more!"

People often asked if we were a Church of Christ. We decided to answer according to the perspective of the questioner. If the inquirer belonged to the Church of Christ, we said, "Yes, in the biblical sense." If the inquirer did not come from the Church of Christ, we responded, "No, not in a denominational sense." Our purpose was positive, however, not negative, and we devoted our time, money and energy to telling others about Jesus and helping the poor.

It is not immodest to say that Sara Faye and I were "pillars" of this little group, along with Mark and Phyllis Whitt, another couple slightly younger than we, who quickly became our closest friends. When the Lord blessed their barbecue business, the Whitts built a new house. In it, Mark included a spacious study, which he soon filled with the best religious books both current and classic.

Through the Elm Street years, Mark was my spiritual "Aaron and Hur," a faithful, steady and constant encourager and fellow laborer for Christ, not only at home but even accompanying me across the country on one occasion to minister to a church in crisis. The hours Sara Faye and I spent together with Mark and Phyllis at table, on our knees, around the Word of God, and in the ordinary activities of life will live forever in my memory and were truly an investment in eternity.

During those years at Elm Street, I researched and wrote *The Fire That Consumes*, a 500-page, scholarly study of the biblical doctrine of final punishment and its later historical development. In God's hand, during two decades since its publication in 1982, that book has helped to stimulate a restudy of the topic by thousands of evangelical Christians around the world. Looking back now, I see that God provided me a special shelter in the Elm Street Church—a safe environment that encouraged independent Bible study and honest historical research.

Although no one spoke in tongues or prophesied in our assemblies, by 1979 Elm Street was inclined toward what, now widespread, was then still considered a "charismatic" worship style—singing Scripture choruses and contemporary songs that addressed God and Christ in the second-person, lifting hands in praise, and openly yearning for God to act directly in our lives and ministry.

I Was Stupid and Blind to My Wife's Needs

Sara Faye and I had changed our thinking together on many topics through the years, but we were not of one mind concerning spiritual gifts. God had given me peace on that subject in 1977, during the day of fasting and prayer in the woods, but my own tranquility did not extend to my wife. Several times, Sara Faye hinted that she could not stand much more change. However, the spiritual adventure both thrilled and invigorated me; even when some of our conversations left my wife in tears, I still did not catch on.

"I feel like I am always running after you," Sara Faye told me later, "and just as I think I've finally caught up, I look up again and you are down the road somewhere else." For the most part, I was oblivious to the anguish my independence caused her, and I was not nearly as sensitive and loving as I should have been concerning her pain which I did perceive.

Those were the circumstances the second time I heard the "still, small voice." It came as I was walking one day during my lunch hour in Decatur, reading a book by the late Chinese evangelist Watchman Nee and praying as I walked. Suddenly I was engulfed with a sense of my wife's pain. Then, as clearly as if someone had spoken aloud, inside my head I heard the clear instruction: "Tell her she's free."

As I considered the command, its meaning became clear. Sara Faye was not obligated to attend church with me. If she needed to go somewhere else for her own spiritual good, it was perfectly permissible for her to do so. The concept directly contradicted my previous opinions, which I had expressed to my wife more than once.

I rushed back to the print shop and called her on the telephone. "Get a baby-sitter for tonight," I said. "We're going out to eat somewhere nice. I have something very important to tell you!" She could not imagine what I had to say that was so significant, and I could not then imagine how powerfully this announcement would impact her. That night I described in detail what had occurred at lunch and the message I had heard. "You are completely free," I said. "I was wrong in the past to insist that we attend church together. God wants you to do whatever you need to do, and I am not to stand in your way."

She burst into tears of joy. "You cannot possibly know how much this means to me," she said. "I have struggled and worried about this for months, but you refused to listen to me or hear what I was trying to say. I had almost decided to leave you, if it took that to get your attention." As it happened, we continued to worship together after all. By the grace of God, we hope to celebrate our 35th wedding anniversary shortly after this book goes to press.

God Also Has a Sense of Humor

The Bible sometimes pictures God as laughing at our mortal foibles. In that light, I must provide him plenty of cause to chuckle. Ever since graduate school, I have longed to teach in college. I was very excited, therefore, when in 1980 the dean of a nearby college invited me to teach a class in creative writing, assuming enough students registered for the course.

I jumped at the chance, but soon questioned my own motives. The earlier message about "You've got the question wrong" was fresh in my mind. Maybe I wanted to do this too much. Could the desire to teach be misdirected? Perhaps God did not want me to teach this class, simply because I coveted the opportunity so strongly. All this was going through my head as I walked again one day during lunch.

As I agonized over these questions, once again I heard the "still, small voice" inside my head. "It doesn't matter if it doesn't matter." What? I puzzled over the cryptic words. Then I smiled as the meaning sunk in. "God is not a killjoy," I thought. "So long as I can submit to God's will about a teaching position—if I can either take it or leave it—he does not care either way."

So What Does all This Prove?

I have heard this inner voice only a few times in my 58 years. Many great saints say they have never heard it. How do we account for that? My first answer is the verse God gave me years ago from Psalm 115. "Our God is in the heavens, and he does whatever he pleases." I do not know why God does or does not do anything. He is sovereign. He does not ask our advice. He does not answer to us.

There is no reason to think such divine communications signify either holiness or spiritual maturity on the part of their recipient. Such communications do seem to correspond to degrees of human desperation or need. God adapts to the situation. He meets people where they are. He does not usually talk through donkeys. But he did once, when a certain man named Balaam was too stubborn or stupid to hear him any other way. God also did what it took to pierce my thick skull with the truth I needed to hear. I am thankful that God is patient and kind, full of mercy and very longsuffering indeed. He has pity on his foolish children, and he reaches out to us however he chooses and as he sees best.

The hymn writer told the truth: "He speaks, and the sound of his voice is so sweet the birds hush their singing." As old Eli charged young Samuel, let us also tune our ears to hear the voice of God. We may join David in praise to God who "opens" our ears, not only once but, as Isaiah pictures it, "morning by morning." Every waking moment our attitude may be: "speak, Lord; your servant is listening."

Whenever we think we do hear that inner voice, we must test its message by Scripture, and by its effect on our lives. If the message passes those tests, we may go forward, trusting the Creator who made us in the first place and who loves us more than we can even imagine.

TO REFLECT OR DISCUSS

1. Edward suggests that God's "inner voice" often comes in times of human desperation or need, and that it is not a sign of holiness or spiritual maturity. What is your reaction to those observations?

2. Do you know anyone who has heard this "inner voice" of God? Under what circumstances did that occur? What effect did it have?

3. The final paragraph of this chapter urges us to test the "inner voice" by the teaching of Scripture, and by the effect of any such message on our lives. Do these tests themselves come from the Scriptures? If so, should they be adequate as tests?

Chapter 9

Wisdom through Godly Counsel

O how kindly has Thou led me,
Heav'nly Father, day by day;
Found my dwelling, clothed and fed me,
Furnished friends to cheer my way!

–Thomas Grinfield

My friend Carl served as dean of Calhoun Community College near Decatur, Alabama, but his roots were firmly planted in the rolling Tennessee hills a few miles to the north. In October 1972, two months after Sara Faye and I moved back to Athens, Carl casually mentioned that his Tennessee father-in-law wished to sell a number of bred cows, and that he was considering buying some of them himself. Calving time was approaching and each new animal should bring a choice price. For a few hundred dollars investment per cow, Carl confided, someone could pick up a tidy profit.

Dreaming of Cattleman Riches
Although I never lived on a farm and knew absolutely nothing about livestock, Carl's comments stuck in my mind. Sara Faye and I were still trying to adjust to a diminished income

after four-and-a-half years of relative affluence in St. Louis with no children and two jobs. Now, with a grand income of $160.00 per week, I certainly could use some easy money. This cow business could be the start of something big! Soon I was envisioning myself as a prosperous gentleman farmer.

The next time I saw Carl, I pursued the subject further. "What kind of cows is your father-in-law selling?" I inquired.

"Charolais."

"Never heard of them."

"They're originally a French breed," Carl explained, "as you can tell from the name."

This information piqued my curiosity even more. "What do they eat?" I asked.

"Absolutely anything," Carl said. "That's what's so good about this breed. They're cheap to feed, almost never get sick, and require practically no attention at all."

"Just the kind of animal for someone who doesn't know anything about cows," I thought. "Or have any pasture. Or have time to tend a herd of cattle."

Being of a practical mindset, however, I knew that cattle-raising involved some down-to-earth details, so I again sought Carl's advice. "What do you do if you live in town and don't have any pasture?" I asked.

"No problem," he said. "You can rent pasture all over this county."

"One other thing," I volunteered. "I really don't have any money."

"Doesn't matter," he replied. "The banks will loan money on these cows."

That was enough for me. Soon the phone lines were humming. As it happened, my neighbor owned a farm about 20 miles out of town. This was surely my lucky day, because he was willing to rent out pasture! Next I called my banker. Yes, he sometimes made loans on livestock, and, yes, I could come work out details once I had rented the pasture. I was ecstatic. God was surely good to me. Soon I would have $1,000.00 or more in clear profit. All I had to do was start the ball rolling, sit back, and wait for the money to come in. That's when I bumped into my good friend Arvid.

An Unwelcome Word of Wisdom

Arvid was nine years older than I. Like myself, he grew up in Limestone County, graduated from Athens Bible School, then attended Florida Christian College and Abilene Christian College. Unlike me, he was reared in the country and usually farmed part-time regardless of his real job. I considered Arvid to be one of my closest and most trusted friends.

He seemed his usual jovial self when we met on the sidewalk in downtown Athens that particular day. "How've you been?" he called out.

"Great!" I said, and excitedly described the profitable bovine venture on which I was about to embark. To my dismay, he did not share my enthusiasm.

"You don't have any land," Arvid pointed out. I explained that I intended to rent pasture.

"You're not a farmer," he continued. I patiently countered that it didn't matter, since these cows ate anything, never got sick, and required practically no care.

Arvid persisted. "All cows get sick. What'll you do when they get hollow-tail?"

"Hollow-tail?"

"And how will you feel when they get through the fence in the middle of the night and someone calls you at 2:00 a.m. to come round them up 20 miles away from home?"

"I hadn't thought of that," I said meekly.

"There are lots of things you haven't thought of, I'll bet," Arvid said. "You don't have any business being a farmer. You don't know anything about it and you'll go broke for sure." I didn't want to hear this, but deep inside I knew he was probably correct.

Disappointed, I called Carl to say that I would not be buying those wonderful cows after all. "No problem," he said. "Arvid is going to buy them all."

Now I was truly indignant. "How could he do this to me?" I thought. "We are supposed to be friends."

About a year later, I met Arvid again one day. My feelings of betrayal had not entirely subsided, and I gingerly raised the subject of the cows.

"You should thank the Lord you didn't buy them," he exclaimed. "You'd have lost your shirt!"

"How's that?"

Several of the cows were not bred, he said, and they never bore calves. Some others contracted a disease and nearly died. If he hadn't owned his own pasture and grown his own hay, Arvid said, he would have lost his entire investment. As it was, he barely broke even.

That evening before sleeping I counted my blessings. "Thank you, Lord!" I exclaimed. "Thank you for the advice I didn't want to hear. You saved me from my own ignorance this time."

Wise People from My Youth

"A man of understanding acquires wise counsel," says the book of Proverbs, supposedly written by the wisest man who ever lived. "A fool," on the other hand, "despises instruction." After the incident of Arvid and the cows, I did not need to be convinced that those aphorisms were true—or that God sometimes guides us through the godly wisdom of others. Reflecting back over my first half-century, I realize that God has given me many such valuable counselors in the form of relatives, teachers and friends.

For my first 18 years, my parents imparted much godly wisdom, by instruction and by example. They did it so constantly and so naturally that I could no more identify it now than I could point to an arm or leg and identify the source of assimilated nutrients from last week's meals.

Since we married in 1967, Sara Faye has contributed regularly to my welfare, often against my protest. Sometimes I have ignored her counsel, but usually to my peril. Her value in this regard has been so obvious to others who knew us that a friend once told me I should make a motto of Genesis 21:12 which says, "Whatever Sarah says to you, listen to her." After more than three decades of marriage, I finally have begun to appreciate the great gift God gave me in my wife's wisdom, both her female intuition in general and her individual insight in particular.

I also reflect with gratitude on the sound counsel of many teachers at Athens Bible School, some of whom still stand out in my mind 40 years later. There was Don Osborne, for example, who was constantly saying, "If you do wrong, you'll get hurt." Good advice and solid wisdom for living, as illustrated every night on the television evening news.

Alma Richter taught me algebra and geometry. Along the way, she also encouraged me to think for myself as a responsible person under God. Mrs. Richter spurred all her students to accomplish our best, urging us to aspire to great things later in life. "You can be whatever you want to be," she told us over and again.

Later, at Florida College, Homer Hailey taught in passing as well as by planned lectures. "Boys," he said, as we read through the Epistle to the Hebrews, "it's an exciting adventure to walk by faith!" He had learned from personal experience what Jesus told Nicodemus, that the believer's life, led by God, is as unpredictable as the wind. He also knew that the believer could face the future unafraid of any contingency, because, as he also liked to say, "One man plus God is a majority." Faith had no limits, he reasoned, "if you spell your God with a capital 'G.'"

Reuel Lemmons' Writing Formula

While a college senior at Abilene, I once visited over lunch with Reuel Lemmons, who for decades edited a Christian paper called *The Firm Foundation*. Starting about age 18, I had submitted articles to editor Lemmons, and he had printed many of them through the years. Now I could ask his advice about writing, face to face.

"I'll tell you how I do it," he said in his jocular manner. "I sit down and write as fast as I can until I have said all I want to say. Then I rewrite it, and rewrite it, and rewrite it, until I have taken out every unnecessary word, and have used the best words I possibly can for whatever is left. I recommend the same process to you."

His advice reminded me of the instructions I once heard for sculpting an elephant: Start with a huge block of stone, then chisel away everything that doesn't look like an elephant. But it was good advice and I have tried to follow it. What you are reading here certainly didn't start out this way, for example, and much of what was on this page in first draft has long since been "blipped" out of existence by the key on my computer which says "Delete."

Friends Who Punctured My Vanity

At Abilene I was studied Greek under Dr. Paul Southern, who also later served on my graduate thesis committee. During oral examinations at the conclusion of the master's degree, Dr. Southern gave me some advice that had far wider application than its literal meaning. At that point, I had completed the equivalent of eight or nine years of Greek. "Don't think you know anything about Greek," the venerable professor counseled, "until you've studied it for at least ten years." There was no magic in the number ten, of course. Still, Dr. Southern's advice demonstrated concretely the New Testament admonition: "If any man thinks he knows anything, he does not yet know as he ought to know."

Much of the best advice I have received has punctured my vanity, reminded me who I am, and brought me down to earth. Sometimes it has come through close friends, who saw me more clearly than I saw myself. Soon after I began preaching for the Church of Christ in Kirkwood, Missouri in 1968, a long-time friend named Don came to our church to conduct a revival.

At age 24, I already had enough books to fill shelves running around three walls in my church study, and the other wall was covered with diplomas and certificates of achievement. I showed Don around the church, then led him to my study to visit. As we discussed the minister's role, I explained that I thought of myself as a sort of theologian-in-residence. I felt horribly unqualified to counsel or evangelize, but fairly competent to dispense biblical information and theoretical insight. I did not yet understand the difference between book knowledge and life experience—or the relative practical value of the two.

Don was not impressed. "Forget that business," he said. "The first thing you should do is to take down all those diplomas and certificates. You've got to hold the hands of little old ladies when they get sick, visit your members when they go to the hospital, care for the people who have trouble or problems. Don't think about being a theologian—be your members' friend."

A fellow-minister in St. Louis named Jerry also helped put me in my place. Jerry was from St. Louis originally, but we had become friends at college in Florida. Now he was back in Missouri, not far from the suburb I called home. One Monday morning he came over to visit. As we entered the rear of the Kirkwood church sanctuary, I spied the large golden ropes draped over the ends of the back pews and suddenly remembered how agitated I had been the day before.

Perhaps Jerry could help me solve a problem, I thought. I recounted my frustration with some members who insisted on sitting in the back pews, despite my strong determination that they should not. First, I had taped signs on the pews asking people to sit in front, but people simply removed the signs and sat in the back pews. When that did not work, I bought these beautiful, gold-colored ropes and laid them over the ends of the off-limit pews. "Surely people will leave the pews empty when they see the ropes," I thought. Wrong. They filled the pews the same as always, simply removing the ropes and walking in.

Obviously, what was needed was more "punch." So I tied the ropes to the pews. Certainly, that would keep these straying members out from where they did not belong. Wrong again. They untied the ropes and sat down.

"What can I do, Jerry?" I implored my slightly older friend. "I don't know how to make the people stay out of these pews and sit closer to the front."

Did Jerry solve my problem? No, he gave me some more advice. "You are not a policeman," he said. "Stop trying to enforce your will on other people. You can't even make people follow God's rules, much less your own. Loosen up and let people make their own decisions about where they want to sit."

Darryl's Insight about God's Guidance

Sometimes God sends us an adviser to help us apply heavenly wisdom to our earthly circumstances. Darryl was just such a counselor, a fellow-believer with whom my path crossed briefly in Alabama in 1980—just as I had to decide whether to continue seeking a livelihood at Decatur Printing Company or whether God had something else in store.

By this time, it seemed very clear that I needed to find some other job—unless God intended for me to get deeper and deeper in debt, an alternative that seemed to contradict the plain teaching of Scripture. I also continued to ask God to place me in a situation that would utilize more fully the abilities and education he had provided already.

I desperately sought divine guidance, but seemingly to no avail. It was as if God were playing "hide and seek" with me, although I knew that he is neither cruel nor capricious and does not treat his children that way. I also struggled with the practical relationship between divine sovereignty and human responsibility. How aggressive should I be in seeking a change? What if God wanted me to stay where I was? Should I simply pray, and wait for him to act? Or did he expect me to make the first move, trusting him to open and close doors as I arrived at each intersection in the path? How might I tell the difference between faith, on the one hand, and presumption, on the other?

While 1 was grappling with these questions late in 1980, I happened to meet Darryl. He was about my age and he immediately impressed me with his down-to-earth faith. One day as we visited over lunch, I shared my struggle with him in learning the right balance between divine sovereignty and human initiative. He thought a moment, then smiled. "I often ask those same questions," he said, "and I'll tell you what someone once told me." I leaned forward, eager to hear some profound truth. "As Christians, we certainly believe that God guides us," he said with a twinkle in his eye, "but have you ever noticed that it is usually easier to guide a moving object?"

That is not always the case, but I felt it was the truth for me at that time. I started moving—while praying earnestly for God to guide the process in keeping with his own best will. For the next twelve months, I searched feverishly for another job, one more consistent with my training and which hopefully might provide a better income than I was earning at the print shop.

I pounded the pavement in Athens and neighboring towns in search of a writing or editing job. I made numerous phone calls and wrote letters to friends around the country. I applied to teach at numerous colleges. I prayed for God to connect me with a compatible church if he wanted me to return to preaching. I also read every "Position Available" notice in the classifieds of *Christianity Today*.

About mid-1981, I saw an advertisement in *Christianity Today* from InterCristo, a Seattle company that matches workers with Christian organizations and ministries around the world. I requested information, completed their detailed questionnaire and paid the fee. Soon InterCristo presented me with several interesting opportunities. One item on the computer printout caught my eye in particular: "Seeking founding editor for interdenominational

Christian newspaper in Houston, Texas." There was a reference person and a post office box number.

I contacted the person listed and one step led to the next. In June of 1982, I moved my family to Houston. There I began *The Good Newspaper*, a tabloid-size biweekly publication that contained only constructive articles. Within three years, it grew to include subscribers in all 50 states.

Out of the Mouths of Babes

My children also have contributed to my "wisification." When we moved to Houston in 1982, the moving van also included over 100 boxes of books—inventory of my publications which I hoped eventually to sell. Five years later, many of the books had sold, but many still remained, stacked almost to the ceiling along one wall of our garage.

By now, our daughter Melanie was 14 and our son Jeremy was 12. We also had Boots the cat. Boots had moved to Texas with us from Alabama, and he loved to explore in unusual places. Occasionally, Boots darted into the garage when a car entered, hid among the boxes of books, and remained behind when we locked the garage. When nature called, lacking sand or other litter, he sometimes used my boxes of books.

One evening after supper, Melanie approached me with a sweet smile. "Daddy," she purred, "what do you want to accomplish with your life?" Pleased that she was thinking so deeply, I launched into a discourse about my dreams and ambitions, all elevated and spiritual in nature. She grinned broadly. "Then does it ever bother you," she asked, "to think that your life's work is stacked in the garage with the cat peeing on it?"

Jeremy also has added perspective to my adult childishness. Shortly after I was licensed to the Bar as an attorney in 1988, he accompanied me one Saturday on some errands about town. When we pulled into a particular strip center, the only parking place available was directly in front of a liquor store. The store's owner had posted a sign that said: "Parking for Liquor Store Customers Only."

"That doesn't matter." I told Jeremy, as I drove into the forbidden parking space. "Under Texas law, we can park anywhere in this strip center we wish, so long as we are visiting some business here."

The engine was still running when the manager came out the door. "You can't park there," he shouted. "Can't you see the sign?"

Very coolly and knowledgeably, I explained to him that I was a lawyer, and that he had no right to put up such a sign. The more I talked, the redder Jeremy's face became and the further he slid down into the seat. When the irate owner proved to be persistent in his demand, I conceded in a grand gesture of noblesse oblige. "I don't have to move," I told him, "but out of courtesy to you I will do so anyway."

As we drove to another place, Jeremy, then 13 years old, finally spoke. "Dad," he said, "I want to give you some advice and you need to follow it. From now on, you be a lawyer when you are at work, and just be a regular person the rest of the time!"

Thank God for Good Advisors

I thank God for my parents, my wife and my children, and for every teacher and friend, who have advised me well. Their important contributions have often kept me from having to learn everything the hard way. God is the source of all true wisdom, whether he sends it directly, by life experience or from other people.

Sometimes God speaks through people who know us well and have first-hand knowledge of what we are going through. But God can also speak powerfully, if he so chooses, through total strangers who are completely ignorant of our circumstances. I learned this in a dramatic way, shortly after we exchanged our familiar Alabama surroundings for an unknown future in cosmopolitan Houston.

TO REFLECT OR DISCUSS

1. Does the story of Carl's cows and Arvid's intervention remind you of any unwelcome advice you ever received that later proved to have been correct?

2. Who is wiser—the person who does not need advice or the person who profits from it?

3. Can you think of biblical examples of God's guiding people through the advice of others?

Chapter 10

Could This Be Prophecy?

Take my voice, and let me sing
Always, only, for my King;
Take my lips, and let them be
Filled with messages from Thee.

–Francis R. Havergal

The move to Texas in 1982 was exciting and frightening at the same time. Melanie was about to begin fourth grade, and she cried at the thought of saying goodbye to childhood friends. Jeremy had just completed first grade, and now wondered apprehensively whether Houston had a McDonald's. Sara Faye grieved to leave our pleasant house, which she had designed and furnished, and its yard blooming with decorative and fruit-bearing trees, lush grapevines, and a rainbow of flowers and shrubs that her Tennessee father had lovingly planted with his own hands.

My anxieties came from the future, as I contemplated finding a house; fashioning from words, ink and paper the newspaper I was hired to start; and locating a church where we could best serve God. Looking back, I also felt a great burden for our brothers and sisters at the Elm Street Church, who had disbanded to find new church homes in different directions. And, while I had always tried to minister God's word honestly and with integrity, new understanding gained over the past decade made me regret some teaching I had done on various topics in earlier years.

Within six months after we arrived in Houston, Sara Faye and I plugged in at the Bering Drive Church of Christ and soon were heavily involved in its various ministries. Unlike some congregations, which select elders for life, Bering elders serve limited terms. In the Spring of 1983, I was one of three new men elected to the eldership. Bering also ordains its designated servants—ministers, elders, missionaries—in a formal ceremony that includes Scripture readings, prayers, responsive promises and commitments, and the laying on of hands.

A Phone Call from Kerry

Two weeks before my ordination as elder, I received a phone call from a long-time friend named Kerry, a Dallas-area businessman and pastor of the Mid-Cities Chapel in Arlington, Texas. "A brother will be ministering here Thursday and Friday nights of next week," Kerry told me, "and I wish you could be present. I believe he exercises a prophetic gift."

At that time, I had never witnessed any contemporary pronouncement that seemed to me to measure up to biblical criteria for prophecy. I was also highly skeptical of anyone who claimed to have that gift. At the same time, I was quite familiar with the Mid-Cities Chapel, and I highly respected Kerry's own biblical knowledge and spiritual maturity.

Several energetic Christian families had formed this congregation a few years before. The elders of a particular Church of Christ had fired their Christ-centered preacher, Hubert, for preaching too clearly our total indebtedness to God's grace. The core of energetic deacons and teachers urged the elders to retract their decision. When they refused, most of the young leaders left, and formed Mid-Cities Chapel.

From the beginning, the brothers and sisters at the Chapel loved each other dearly and eagerly shared Christ with their neighbors. Their joyful lifestyle soon attracted non-Christian seekers, as well as believers from a wider Christian spectrum. As they sought God's presence and studied the Bible together, the Chapel members became increasingly open to the Holy Spirit, and God continued to bless them individually and as a body.

I had been privileged to preach Christ during special meetings at both congregations—first at the original Church of Christ, then at Mid-Cities Chapel after its formation and at regular intervals throughout its development. Once when I returned home after speaking at Mid-Cities Chapel, I felt that the Lord wanted me to destroy all remaining copies of a little book I had written years before which denied that God still bestows the spiritual gifts of tongues. Even though many of the booklet's cautions were appropriate, its dogmatic conclusion contradicted God's word to me a few years earlier through the Scripture which said: "Our God is in the heavens, and he does whatever he pleases." Acting on my inner conviction, I tossed the remaining 2,200 copies in the dumpster.

Under Kerry's leadership, the Chapel members focused on Christ and emphasized practical obedience and witnessing, while they incorporated a constructive use of whatever spiritual gifts God saw fit to bestow. Because of Kerry's faithful ministry and credibility, he seized my attention immediately when he telephoned me that spring evening in 1983.

"Who is this man?" I asked.

"His name is Bill Roycroft." Kerry said. "He lives in Canada, where he operates a Christian outreach for troubled teens. Once or twice a year, he travels through Oklahoma and Texas and speaks at a few congregations with whom he is acquainted. He has been to Mid-Cities Chapel several times now, and I believe you will be blessed by coming."

A Flying, Turn-around Trip

My calendar indicated a busy Friday that next week. I could make this fast trip, but it would mean flying to Dallas after work on Thursday for the evening service and catching the "red-eye" return flight home. I booked my flight and entered the next week with great anticipation.

Thursday afternoon arrived and Kerry met me at the Dallas airport. We grabbed a fast bite en route to the church and arrived just before the evening service. When the time came to begin, the announced speaker still had not arrived, and the presiding brother suggested that we extend our period of praise. We sang five or six more worship songs before the front door opened and the scheduled guest came in. His car's transmission had broken as he drove through Oklahoma, he explained, and he had spent half a day arranging repairs.

Kerry said a few words to introduce Mr. Roycroft and sat down. The speaker was conservative in both style and appearance. "Please turn with me to Genesis." he began, "as we look together again at the familiar story of Joseph."

My mind traveled more than 30 years back to Athens Bible School, where many a chapel speaker had extolled Joseph's virtues and had praised his persistent faith. It seemed fitting to reflect on him again, here in this church called a "Chapel." So, in the conversational tone of one accustomed to small audiences, Mr. Roycroft read excerpts from the Old Testament text, applied a few points to our circumstances, and exhorted us to live faithful lives before our faithful and all-knowing God.

Simply Encouraging One-on-One

Then he began speaking to specific people in the assembly. Just calmly talking, as if one-on-one. He did not announce what he was about to do—or say what he had done when he finished. He never used the word "prophecy." He did not claim to be a prophet. He simply spoke to various individuals, men and women, of different ages and races and circumstances—encouraging this one, consoling another, building them all up in the Lord.

Mr. Roycroft did not know these people and he had not talked with them in advance. He arrived at the meeting after the service had begun. Still he spoke intimately, as if he knew the secret struggles and hidden burdens of each heart, yet carefully, to protect the confidence as a sacred trust. "You, the brother on the right with the red tie," he might say, "you wonder how you can continue to serve the Lord and carry the weight you have had to carry these past years. The Lord would say to you that he knows what you have borne, and he will always be with you. Have courage and continue as you are doing, and God will never leave your side. Live in his strength."

He addressed no one judgmentally but spoke with great compassion to all, delivering kind words in a tender manner. "The Lord would say to the sister in the front row with the blue dress," he began, "you are in great confusion as a new believer, because you feel pulled in opposing directions in your life. God has given you shepherds in the church. Listen to their wisdom and receive their guidance. They care for your soul and love you in the Lord. Trust their loving leadership as one would trust a father."

Among those present were the Church of Christ preacher who had been fired years before for faithfully preaching the grace of Christ, and his hard-working and sacrificial wife. Mr. Roycroft spoke to them both in turn, and each wept tears of joy and great release.

"You have worked very hard for God," Mr. Roycroft told the minister's wife. "You have often given and given to others until you had nothing left to give. You have great reward in heaven, and God will strengthen you now with his daily power for each task that he places before you."

He also encouraged her husband. "You have been abused and persecuted," he acknowledged, "and the Lord would say to you that you have suffered for him. He first suffered for you, and he suffers with you when you suffer in his name." He said more, and these are not his exact words, but they were such words as these.

He talked for about 30 minutes to ten or twelve people in the same manner, and then he stopped. There were no final words to the audience this time. We were almost eavesdroppers. The last half hour had been intended for the specific individuals who had been addressed; the blessing we received was real but secondary. Someone led a benediction and we were dismissed.

I had wept, too, as he spoke to my minister friend and his wife. I knew their histories, though Mr. Roycroft did not, and I sensed divine knowledge and empathy in his words to them. The entire experience had moved me deeply. But now I was terribly disappointed as well. He had not spoken to me.

"Why Did He Turn off the Faucet?"

I made my way through the audience and found Kerry. "Why did he turn off the faucet before everyone got watered?" I asked. Kerry smiled. "Sometimes he has more to say later. Stand here and I'll ask if he does tonight." He walked over to Mr. Roycroft and apparently asked a question. Then, turning toward me, he motioned for me to go into a classroom.

Kerry and his wife Kara followed. They brought three other people with them. The first was a young Nigerian student who was attending university in Arlington. The other two were my friends Mary and Randy, a married couple who were leaving the next day as missionaries with Wycliffe Bible Translators. Mr. Roycroft also came into the classroom.

"Sometimes there is more ministry after the larger group is dismissed." Kerry said simply. "I have asked our brother if he has anything further to say."

He did have more to say, first to the Nigerian student, then to the Bible translators. I did not know their hearts or private spiritual journeys, of course, but they each did. Like the others before them that evening, they responded as if the words spoken met them exactly where they were.

Finally this quiet and unpretentious guest speaker looked at me. "The Lord would say to you," he began, "that as you enter into a new area of ministry, the Lord has gone before you and prepared the way. You do not need to repeat words to your people," he continued. "They have heard so many words their hearts are like a well-worn path. The Lord has given you a listening heart, and he would have you to listen and to love, to minister and to care."

He also spoke about my past. "Do not be concerned for those you have left behind," he encouraged, "for the Lord is also with them, and he will carry out his plans for each of them just as he has purposed. And do not be anxious concerning teaching you have done in years gone by," he said, "for the Lord would say to you that he knows your heart, that you have walked in sincerity before him, and that you have given to others the truth which he had given to you. Now the Lord would encourage you to continue to speak the truth that you know, and to leave the seed you have planted to his care."

Someone took me back to the airport and I returned to Houston, carrying a cassette tape Kerry had made for me as Mr. Roycroft spoke. I was so awed I could barely sleep. I wanted to share details with Sara Faye. Yet, knowing how even the mention of certain spiritual gifts instantly aroused her fear and anxiety, I hesitated to tell her what had actually occurred. When I left for work Friday morning, I placed the tape on the kitchen counter. "This is what the man told me," I said to her. "I don't know if you want to hear it or not. If you do, it is here."

When I returned home that evening, she brought up the subject. "I listened to the tape," she said.

"What did you think about it?"

"It was beautiful," she replied. "I cried all the way through it. He talked as if he knew everything that is going on in your life."

At this point I still had one nagging unanswered question. I picked up the telephone and called Kerry. "Please don't be insulted," I said, "but I have to ask you one question."

He chuckled. "I know what it is," he replied. "It's the same question everyone asks. But go ahead and inquire for your own peace of mind."

"What did you tell Mr. Roycroft last night about me?" I inquired. "I want to know exactly everything that you said."

"Just a couple of sentences," Kerry replied. "I told him that you were from Houston and that you had to return that night. And I asked him if he had anything to say to you before you left. That is all I said."

That Sunday at Bering Drive, three of us were ordained as elders. All the present and former elders placed their hands on us and offered prayers on our behalf. Throughout the service, I thought of the passage in Timothy that says: "Do not neglect the gift that is in you, which was given you by prophecy and by the laying on of the hands of the presbytery." I marveled at God's graciousness. "Prophecy on Thursday night, and the laying on of hands on Sunday," I reflected. "What a responsibility I have to fulfill this charge!" I asked God for strength and faith for the task he had given me to do.

What is Biblical Prophecy, Anyway?

Was Mr. Roycroft exercising the spiritual gift of prophecy? If "our God is in the heavens and he does whatever he pleases," that is a question I must ask. What is the gift of Christian prophecy anyway? Does it mean telling the future? Does it always, or even usually, result in new books of the Bible? As I search the Scriptures. I must answer "No" to both questions.

As frequently noted, the biblical word "prophecy" does not mean "fore-telling" but "forth-telling." Prophecy is simply a direct message from God, spoken through some individual he sees fit to use. Both Old and New Testaments mention many people who delivered God's word—usually to a particular person or group, for a definite purpose, under specific circumstances.

Although God gave these specific messages, they often were not intended for general distribution. The Bible includes some of these prophetic utterances and omits others. On the other hand, the Bible includes many stories and words spoken by people who never communicated a message directly from God. We may therefore draw two conclusions: first, that prophecy frequently does not result in new Scripture; second, that Scripture contains much that is not prophecy.

The New Testament mentions a number of ordinary men and women who prophesied, but who never wrote any Scripture. Before Jesus was born there were Elizabeth and Zachariah. During Jesus' infancy, we meet holy Simeon in the Temple. Even the wicked high priest Caiaphas prophesied concerning Jesus' death. The Book of Acts introduces us to Agabus, to Judas and Silas, to Philip's four daughters and to 12 disciples at Ephesus. All of these believers prophesied on occasion, but none of them wrote any Scripture.

Paul places prophecy at the top of the list of ministry gifts to be desired, even as he insists that not all believers will ever prophesy. It is all in God's sovereign hands—God who distributes different gifts to various believers just as he pleases.

If prophecy is not intended to result in new Scripture, what is its purpose? The 14th chapter of First Corinthians says more about prophecy in the church than all the rest of the Bible combined, and it identifies three goals of this spiritual gift. The person who properly exercises the gift of prophecy edifies, exhorts and consoles. Or, to put it in regular language, he or she "builds up" others to Christian maturity, "stirs up" someone to godly action, or spiritually "binds up" a person who is spiritually weak, broken, or torn down.

Does God Still Speak through People?

But whom does God use to deliver such a word? The answer must surely be, "Whomever he pleases to use." Moses once expressed a wish that all God's people might prophesy, because in his day prophecy was limited to a very few chosen individuals. But the time would come when God would speak to his people on a much broader scale. This is made clear in the opening remarks of the first Christian sermon reported in the Book of Acts.

On the festive Day of Pentecost described in Acts chapter two, Peter quotes Joel's prophecy concerning the "last days." At that time, God promised to "pour out his Spirit on all flesh." One result, according to Joel, would be that "your sons and your daughters will prophesy." Peter informed the astonished crowd that the long-awaited "last days" had now begun. That meant, according to Joel's prophecy, that "whoever calls on the name of the Lord shall be saved." Peter declared Jesus to be that Lord and Christ. But the fact that the "last days" had begun meant something else. It meant that God was ready to speak, more freely than ever before, through ordinary men and women who had no special credentials or titles.

But what did the biblical gift of prophecy look like? How can we recognize it if we see it today? Does Scripture provide us any guidelines or tests for assessing a prophecy? Here we need to forget the special effects of Hollywood and focus instead on the Word of God. Throughout Scripture, the person giving God's word is not usually frenzied or in a trance. He or she is not emotionally overwrought or out of control. That may characterize false prophets and pagan revelations, but it does not describe the prophetic ministry among Christians—in biblical times or today. The prophetic word is a straightforward human word in every mechanical sense. What makes it unique is its origin. God reveals this word directly to the speaker.

The Bible Provides Many Tests

The Apostle Paul warns us not to quench or extinguish the Spirit, or to regard prophecies lightly. He commands us to examine everything, to retain what is good and to reject evil in every form. There are many false prophets in the world. John warns. Christians are not to be gullible or naive. We are to test the spirits—and any message that purports to originate with God.

The last book of the Bible tells us that "the testimony of Jesus is the spirit of prophecy." When the Spirit comes, Jesus had said, "he will glorify me." The true gift of prophecy always exalts Jesus Christ and inspires greater faith in him. Anyone speaking by the Spirit of God will acknowledge that Jesus is Lord. Whoever says otherwise is a false prophet.

True prophecy always agrees with God's revelation given in Scripture. Any so-called prophecy that contradicts the Bible is wrong. It is as simple as that. We need not fear being misled by a David Koresh, whose early teachings directly opposed God's clear and unequivocal commandments, clearly marking him as a false prophet.

A God-inspired word is also recognizable by its effects. As we have already seen, its purpose is to build up, stir up and bind up the body of Christ. This gift is not usually intended for chastising or condemning, or for issuing new commands that the recipient did not already know. Most modern "prophets" fail this test as soon as they start speaking, including all those who say: "God told me to tell you to send me money!" Apparently such hucksters have a long history. One Christian author in the second century warned that anyone who asks for money is a false prophet.

Do We Quench the Spirit?

Scripture encourages us to hospitality by holding out the possibility that we might entertain angels without knowing it. In a similar way, I believe we ought always to speak godly words, with the realization that some of them might spring directly from

God. How often have you thought of some word of encouragement, exhortation, or solace, which you felt you should say to someone else—then you quenched the Spirit by never communicating the word?

How frequently have you been encouraged by the well-spoken word of another person at the moment you needed to hear it most? How many times have you found new strength from a timely word of exhortation, to keep going when you thought you couldn't take another step? Or felt your heart rise with new hope, from the depths of depression, when someone said just the "right" word? Where did those godly words originate? Why were they were so effective in Christ's service? Might they not have been, without our knowing it, words of prophecy?

Spanning two decades in my own life, God used two Christian ladies—Mary Alice Ciampa, in St. Louis, Missouri, and Maude Miller, in Athens, Alabama—to encourage me with such specific words. These godly women, mothers of faith, rekindled my hope in many dark hours, as they repeatedly assured me that God had a future for me which could be neither understood in the midst of, nor ultimately hindered by, the circumstances then present. In the same way, my mother's frequent words of affirmation have encouraged me at just the right times for very many years. I will not be surprised if, in glory, God informs me that all these ladies were exercising a prophetic ministry. I do not know if such a revelation would surprise them or not.

One thing is sure. When Jesus returns, prophecy will end. There will be no further need for it then, since we all will speak with him face to face. Until then, even our lips, consecrated to God, may be filled with messages from the loving heavenly Father. If you feel you have a good word for someone—say it! Who knows but that God has given it to you for them? After all, "our God is in the heavens, and he does whatever he pleases."

Another Divine Word—of Knowledge

The prophetic word is not the only divine word mentioned in the New Testament. God also sometimes gives a word of knowledge, or a word of wisdom. These supernatural gifts mean just what they sound like, "knowledge" and "wisdom." But this knowledge is not learned by normal human means, and this wisdom shortcuts all usual processes for gaining insight.

Both gifts overlap at times with the prophetic word. It is very possible, for example, that God gave Mr. Roycroft a word of knowledge about my personal circumstances, a word of wisdom about my spiritual and emotional need, and prophetic words to meet those needs.

I do not think we can be dogmatic in defining these overlapping gifts too strictly. It is far less important to analyze and to name a particular gift than it is to use it in love to the glory of God. That was my earnest desire a few years ago when, I believe, God told me the name of the stranger sitting beside me on an airplane high in the skies over Texas.

It was a Sunday afternoon in November, 1996. I had flown from my home in Houston to Tucson, Arizona that weekend, to preach at an independent church in the tiny desert town of Oracle. Now, ministry completed, I looked forward to a few restful hours traveling home. Traffic was unusually heavy in Tucson, however, and I almost missed the flight. At the airport, I rushed to the American Airline ticket counter, and then ran to the departure gate as fast as my stubby, out-of-shape body could move. Last to board the plane, I found my aisle seat and fastened in. The schedule said 2 1/2 hours to Dallas, where I was to change planes for a final 45-minute hop home to Houston.

The lady beside me was wearing jeans. However, her hair, jewelry and manner all suggested that she was a business or professional woman, probably of comfortable means. I wondered if she was Jewish. (Later, I learned that she was not. I certainly have no natural ability to analyze strangers.) She was dozing when I sat down. I opened the book I had begun on my trip to Arizona, a stimulating volume entitled *Surprised by the Voice of God.* The author was Jack Deere, formerly a professor at Dallas Theological Seminary. As I resumed reading, Deere described how God sometimes reveals a word or phrase to his children that they would not otherwise know. Yet this very word—oftentimes a name—enhances ministry to another person for whom it has special meaning.

Silently, I offered myself to God for ministry to the lady beside me. If he wished to give me a word or phrase for that purpose, I said, I was willing to be stretched – although nothing like that had ever happened to me before. Immediately, the name "Karen" came to my mind, and with considerable force. My neighbor was not wearing any initial jewelry and she did not resemble anyone I knew by that name. Still the thought persisted. "Karen."

"Is that her name?" I asked myself. How awesome it would be, I thought, if God had actually given me her name. But what if I had merely imagined it? Did I dare say anything to her? If I were wrong, she would surely think this was an unusual, if creative, "line."

I argued back and forth with myself for a half-hour, perhaps 45 minutes, as I continued to read, glimpsing periodically at my neighbor, now wide awake, neither of us saying anything or making eye contact. Should I speak to her or not? What would she think? Would it be presumptuous? But what if God had told me this name? If, through fear or timidity, I did not say something to her, I would never know.

About an hour-and-a-half into the flight, no words yet spoken between us, we flew over Abilene's lights far below. At this point, my companion was looking out the window. Finally I spoke. "There's a city," I volunteered. "It must be Abilene."

"Yes," she replied.

"I have a daughter who lives there and teaches elementary

music," I added. She smiled. "You had better tell her hello." I waved toward the window and said, "Hello, Melanie!"

Suddenly, screwing up my courage, I blurted out, "Your name wouldn't happen to be Karen, would it?"

Obviously startled, she looked directly at me for the first time. "As a matter of fact," she replied, "it is. How did you know that?"

"I think God just told me," I replied, realizing she might conclude that I was deranged. "I am a lawyer and a Bible teacher," I explained. "I have been out in the desert preaching at a little church. And I was just sitting here reading a book about learning to hear God's voice. I asked God, if he wanted me to encourage you, to tell me something about you, and the name 'Karen' came to mind. Do you need any encouragement in any area of your life?"

"Not that I can think of," she said. "Actually, things are going very well for me right now. I have just visited my daughter and her family in Tucson. Her name is Karen also."

We conversed all the way to Dallas—not surprisingly, about God. Karen told me that she was Lutheran by birth, attended a Baptist church, and was very committed personally to the Lord. A single breadwinner and young grandmother, she worked for a Los Angeles company whose cosmetic products she merchandised to grocery chains throughout the state of Texas. As we talked about God's faithfulness and power, she confided, "I don't know how I could make it through life without God. I depend on him in every part of my life."

At that point, we descended into Dallas. As we parted company, we both were laughing with joy at what had happened, marveling at the God who loves each of us so intimately—the heavenly Father who even knows our names.

TO REFLECT OR DISCUSS

1. Have you usually linked the biblical gift of prophecy to the writing of Scripture? How do the New Testament's own examples of Christian prophecy fit that understanding?

2. Would you appreciate receiving prophetic ministry such as that described in this chapter? Why or why not?

3. Some people fear that any modern prophecy threatens the authority of Scripture itself. Do the tests Edward proposes here adequately resolve that concern?

4. Can you think of any time in your own life when it seemed that God spoke to you through another believer? Did you ever sense that God spoke through you to someone else?

Chapter 11

Obey—God Is at Work!

Perhaps today there are loving words
which Jesus would have me speak;
There may be now in the paths of sin
some wand'rer whom I should seek;
O Savior, if Thou wilt be my guide,
tho' dark and rugged the way,
My voice shall echo Thy message sweet,
I'll say what you want me to say.

–Mary Brown

I scanned the faces of the 50 or so people sitting around me on three sides, searching for any suggestion of openness or warmth—some human reflection of the spring that surrounded us outdoors. Instead, I saw only pain and sorrow, in countenances as bleak and stony as the nonsectarian Rothko Chapel in Houston where we had gathered to pay final respects to Mike. Such mournful assemblies had become a familiar ritual to many of those assembled, as death rapidly diminished their closest circle of acquaintances and friends.

Sara Faye and I had driven to the memorial service with Bob and Beth, a young married couple from our church. Apparently, we four heterosexuals were part of a very small minority on this particular occasion in 1990.

The printed program indicated that seven men and women would reminisce about the deceased, who had died of AIDS a few weeks before. "Mike had a lot of anger," one close friend reflected. "We all caught it at one time or another, but we always knew that he loved us." Mike was a real "hell-raiser," if his friends were to be believed. In fact, once this meeting ended, the presider informed us, we all were invited to a party. "Mike would like for us to do that in his honor," he explained. There was no mention of God, no word of hope, no anticipation of the hereafter.

"Give Me the Heart and Words . . ."

"We do not know the next speaker," the presider said, about midway through the program. "I have talked with him one time on the telephone. But we do know the change we saw in Mike the last few weeks of his life. Those of us who were close to him know that he experienced something very profound a couple of months ago—something so meaningful to him that, from then until he died, he wanted to talk of nothing else. It happened during a visit he had with our next speaker. Because of the life-changing impact that conversation had on Mike, I have asked Mr. Fudge to come and tell us whatever it was he told Mike."

As I went forward, I was thinking of Paul's words to the Philippians: "Work out your own salvation with fear and trembling; for it is God who is at work in you, both to will and to do his good pleasure." Fear and trembling. I could certainly relate to that. "I don't know what you have in mind here today, Lord," I prayed silently, "but I know you are in charge and I ask you to give me the heart and words which you can use to your glory."

Bob and Beth Showed Jesus' Love

God had already used Bob and Beth, the real heroes in this story and my fellow-members at the Bering Drive Church of Christ in Houston. Some time before, they had hired a house painter and Mike had come along to help. Along the way, they befriended this gentle gay man in his early 30's. They did not know it, but Mike already carried the HIV virus throughout his slender frame.

When Bob and Beth heard that Mike had AIDS, they responded with caring concern. As his disease progressed to its final stages, Mike, now blind and emaciated, entered a neighborhood hospice to die. Bob and Beth continued to share Christ's love through phone calls and personal visits. Beth went to see Mike almost every day, frequently taking him lunch or dinner. One day their silent witness bore fruit. "I know I am about to die," Mike told them. "Do you know someone I can talk to about God?"

Modestly under-rating their own ability to communicate the gospel message, Bob and Beth called Bill, our preacher, and explained the situation to him. Bill was about to leave for speaking appointments in another state, so he phoned me at the law office downtown and asked if I would visit Mike. I agreed to go, then called Bob and Beth for more information. Then I telephoned Mike to arrange a convenient time to visit. "God, give me words and wisdom," I beseeched as I drove to Omega House. "I certainly do not know what to say or how to say it."

A friendly volunteer met me at the door of the 50's-style bungalow. "I have come to visit Mike," I explained. "He is expecting me." There were two other dying men at Omega House besides Mike, and I greeted them as I walked past their open doors. I wondered if they could detect that inside I was scared stiff. The volunteer led me into Mike's bedroom. "Mike," she said cheerily, "You have a visitor. This is Mr. Fudge."

"Hello, Mike," I said. His sightless eyes turned toward the sound of my voice. Barely 30 years old, he looked more like 90, a living skeleton shrouded in pale skin curled in a fetal position on top of the bed covers. "Hello, Mr. Fudge," he replied. "I'm glad that you came." His voice was surprisingly strong.

"I'm a friend of Bob and Beth," I explained, as if he didn't know. We chatted small talk for a few minutes before turning to the point of the visit. "Tell me about your past experience with

God," I invited. "Have you ever known the Lord in a personal way?"

"Yes," he said. His voice grew softer. "When I was a boy in Georgia, my mother was a Christian and she took us all to Baptist Sunday School. At about age 13, I accepted Christ as my Savior and was baptized. When I went away to college, though, I kind of left all that, and my life went a different direction. I haven't had much to do with God since then."

"We are all sinners, Mike," I told him, "just in different respects. But God loves us more than we can ever know, and he came in the person of Jesus Christ to die for our sins and bring us back to himself." Jesus' story of the Prodigal Son came to mind just then. I told it again to Mike, noting that God is like the father who waits day after day for his lost children to return, and who eagerly runs to welcome them when they finally do come home.

"We can never earn God's love or forgiveness," I added. "We can only receive it by faith, trusting in what Jesus did on the cross to set us right with God. You have told me that you once knew God as your Father, but for many years you have been away from home. According to Jesus, God is ready right now to receive you and to keep you with him forever. He will do that, if you are genuinely sorry for your sins and sincerely ask him to forgive you. Is that what you want to do?"

As a former minister, I had visited people many times who were sick or in distress. Church members usually asked the preacher to pray, and I expected Mike to do the same. But this prayer was too intimate for a stranger's words, too personal for anyone else to express.

"Yes." Mike said, and he began praying aloud. As he prayed, he wept softly, then louder, finally sobbing in great convulsions, pouring out his heart to the Father who welcomes his lost children home. I wept also, with fear and trembling, knowing that this was holy ground.

God Transformed Mike's Life

I really intended to go back and visit Mike, but somehow I never did. A few weeks later, Beth told me he had died. Then one day the telephone rang at my office. A voice on the other end asked, "Are you the man who talked with Mike about God?" I acknowledged that I was, and my caller continued.

"I don't know if you knew it or not," he said, "but whatever you told Mike changed his life dramatically. From that day forward, he was full of joy and hope and peace—almost like he was a new person. Several of his friends are meeting at Rothko Chapel next Saturday in his honor. Some of us who knew him best will be making a few remarks. Could you come tell us what you told Mike, that made such a difference in his life?"

And so we went—Bob and Beth, and Sara Faye and myself—and they offered up silent prayers while I told Mike's friends the good news that sustained him through his final days and into the world beyond. At the first mention of God, most eyes glazed over. However, a few cheeks glistened with tears, and I wondered what history those men and women had with God and what God might be doing this day in that place.

The Audience from B'nai B'rith

It was another Saturday the same year, but the circumstances and surroundings could hardly have been more different. Yet I knew that God was at work here, too, as I looked around the conference table at 15 Jewish leaders from six southern states. We were at the Houstonian, the elite hotel and health resort that then-President George Bush and wife Barbara officially designated as their Texas residence.

The mounted video camera hummed softly as Alan, the host, introduced me to his seminar participants. "Our speaker for this session is a Houston attorney I have come to respect," he began. "Edward will address us for about 45 minutes on the Bible from a Christian perspective, then take your questions for the remainder of this two-hour session."

We had met a year earlier, Alan and I, when we faced off on opposite sides of a multi-million dollar lawsuit. As an associate with a major Texas law firm, I represented the Federal Deposit Insurance Corporation (FDIC), which sued a prominent Houston businessman who had defaulted on a long-term commercial lease.

The businessman hired Alan to represent him, and he was well represented. Alan was the principal partner of a prestigious, specialized law firm in the city, and he had practiced much longer than I. We were about the same age, however, and we felt a strong and instant rapport. We discovered rather quickly that we both were men of faith, this Jewish man and I. Soon we were lingering after depositions to discuss our personal and spiritual lives.

Despite Alan's far greater experience as an attorney, I had an enormous advantage in the lawsuit. Under federal law, his client could not even talk about certain facts in this case, details that might have excused his conduct totally under normal circumstances. Even a skilled attorney such as Alan was practically helpless in this situation.

He was not surprised, therefore, when my client prevailed, but Alan did say that he was surprised by something else. "I greatly appreciate the way you dealt with my client," he said. "You could have humiliated him and ruined him for life. Instead, you treated him in a decent and humane manner which allowed him to preserve his dignity."

One day during these proceedings, Alan broached a subject he seemingly regarded as sensitive. "As an officer of B'nai B'rith," he said, "I am in charge of a program called New Horizons." A little smile tugged at the corners of his mouth. "Each year we bring a dozen or so promising Jewish men from several states to Houston for an intensive weekend of leadership training," he continued.

He explained that these participants were chosen to represent a cross-section of Jewish community leaders—doctors, businessmen, accountants and lawyers. The weekend program was equally varied, including presentations on medicine, business, law, communications, management, finance, religion and other practical topics.

"I wonder if you would be willing to come to our next seminar and talk about the Bible from a Christian perspective."

Without hesitation, I accepted the invitation and immediately began to pray and to think about what I should say.

I knew that Jews today generally consider most Western Gentiles to be Christians, including those such as the Crusaders and later the Nazis who persecuted Jews. Because of this historical baggage, modern rabbis regularly insist that "Jewish" and "Christian" are mutually exclusive terms. So far as they are concerned, any Jew who accepts Jesus as Messiah automatically ceases to be a Jew.

Now I Asked God for Words

Alan finished his introduction and the camera focused on me. "As a Christian," I began, "I owe a great debt to the Jews. I come before you today as a wild Gentile branch grafted on to the original Jewish plant. I do not come here to represent Christendom, or any Christian denomination, or what you might consider cultural Christianity. I do not ask you to give up anything that is authentically Jewish, or ask you to accept anything contrary to the Hebrew Scriptures."

I acknowledged that modern rabbis deny that a Jew can believe in Jesus and remain Jewish. I also told these men that was a relatively new notion, and that it contradicted their own Bible and historical reality. I pointed out that Jesus himself was a Jew, as were his Apostles and all his earliest followers. I explained that, except for Luke and Acts, all the New Testament books were written by Jews.

I prayed much and studied long before coming to this meeting, but now I spoke extemporaneously as the words came to my mind. I began with the first verse of the Bible, which I quoted in the original Hebrew language that these American Southerners all read and spoke. Then I told the story of redemption—of Paradise, the Fall, the Flood, and God's call to Abraham and his descendants after him.

For 45 minutes I summarized the mighty acts of God, from Genesis to Malachi. I explained that the Hebrew Bible, which Christians revere as their Old Testament, presents an unfinished symphony. Its themes of sacrifice and priesthood, of divine revelation, of messianic hope and the kingdom of God, all are completed and fulfilled in the story of Jesus of Nazareth. Jesus lived and loved and healed the sick, I noted. The Romans, cheered on by the jealous priestly Sadducees, executed him on a cross. But on the third day afterward, Jesus rose from the dead—in keeping with the Hebrew Scriptures.

Every eye was attentive as I drew to the close. "As we leave here today," I said, "and through the years to come, I urge you to consider that Jesus of Nazareth is the Messiah foretold by your ancient prophets. He is the fulfillment of every ideal, dream and aspiration of all the Hebrew Scriptures."

During the question-answer session that followed, I was as surprised by what these Jewish men did not ask as by what they did ask. Not one denied that Jesus lived, or worked miracles, or even that he arose from the dead. No one seriously disputed his miraculous conception, although they did not necessarily accept it.

They were troubled by the idea of the Trinity, a concept that even Christians have great difficulty explaining in practical and understandable terms. They strongly questioned the idea that God somehow became human in a specific historical person, and especially that the suffering of one man could atone for the sin of another. Perhaps most of all, they were scandalized by the continued presence of evil and injustice. "If Jesus is the Messiah," they asked, "why do we not see the Golden Age promised by the prophets?"

The Mystery of God's Workings

I do not know exactly what God had in mind at the memorial service at Rothko Chapel that day—or at the Jewish seminar at the Houstonian. But I am confident that God knows, and that his word "will not return to him void." I also know that I could never have imagined, in all my preceding years, some day sharing the gospel with either audience.

What is most thrilling is the realization that the heavenly Father used simple obedience in the daily lives of ordinary people to bring about both opportunities. Bob and Beth had no specific agenda when they showed love to Mike. They simply made themselves available to Christ and his love overflowed through them. I was not attempting to evangelize when I represented the FDIC in its suit against Alan's client. I tried only to conduct myself in a Christian manner that would honor God.

In a day when we are often obsessed with methods and programs, with organized plans and specialized activities, we need to remember that God's power is still the only force which can draw women and men to Jesus Christ. Most often, God accomplishes his purpose through the mundane affairs of his people, as they attempt to obey him in the small details of daily life.

Learning to Watch and Pray

Nor do we need to wait for unusual audiences such as the two I have described in this chapter in order to share the gospel. These are extreme examples. I relate them only to illustrate that there is no person God cannot reach, no group he does not love. I have been a very slow learner, but it has been a great blessing to me in recent years to discover that opportunities to witness await us almost every day—on the street, at the job, during a doctor's visit, over the coffee table or in the middle of a round of golf.

As we live close to God, he will make our paths intersect with others who he knows are seeking him. If we live prayerfully, and keep alert, we can see openings for planting gospel seed, and, in

God's strength and wisdom, take advantage of them to his glory. We do not need to worry about results. It is our job to be faithful in small details, and then to be ready to speak as God gives opportunity. We may be sure that God will accomplish whatever pleases him. And—wonder of wonders—sometimes he uses people like us!

TO REFLECT OR DISCUSS

1. Does it surprise you to hear that God carries out his saving purpose through the normal course of our daily lives?

2. How might we become more aware of divine opportunities to be God's agents? What if Bob and Beth had ignored Mike because they were not trained evangelists?

3. Do you feel the need to see the results of God's work through you, or can you happily serve as he directs and leave the outcome to God?

4. Are you willing to ask God each day to use you to touch others, in whatever way God might see fit?

Chapter 12

Open and Closed Doors

All the way my Savior leads me;
What have I to ask beside?
Can I doubt his tender mercy,
Who thro' life has been my Guide?

—Fanny J. Crosby

Looking back over the past fifty-eight years, it is fairly easy now to see God's hand sovereignly leading, clearly visible in retrospect, at every major intersection along the way. My constant companion, he was always there—silently blazing a trail, arranging circumstances, timing events and people according to his own purposes.

When Sara Faye and I married in 1967, an ensemble at our wedding sang the hymn "Savior, Like a Shepherd Lead Us." We were thrilled to see God do just that a year later in providing my first job. We both assumed that I would preach, but the likelihood of finding a church that might want me appeared very slim. Somehow, it seemed, I was often a square peg in a round hole.

A Square Peg in a Round Hole

At Florida College I had advocated broader views of grace and fellowship than those held by many of my associates.

Because of this, some influential preachers in those circles spread the word that I was "leaning toward Ketcherside." This was a reference to St. Louis author and preacher W. Carl Ketcherside, who had been a reformer among Churches of Christ for many years. His offense? Why, he had the audacity to plead that our various factions ought to find "unity in diversity." And he insisted on recognizing as brothers and sisters all who were children of God.

At Abilene Christian College, I was viewed with suspicion because I came from Florida College, which represented a splinter group among Churches of Christ. Now I was ready to seek a pulpit among that splinter group of churches, but its leaders considered me liberal because I had studied at Abilene. Was there a church anywhere that would choose me?

There was not a lot of time to spare, either. Sara Faye and I had married after college graduations in June of 1967, then moved to Abilene in August for my graduate program in biblical languages. As I worked to complete my thesis during the Summer of 1968, I knew that I faced joblessness unless a door of opportunity opened within a few weeks.

As it happened, a year or two before, Dan and Jeanie, long-time family friends in Athens, Alabama, had been transferred to Kirkwood, Missouri, a lovely, western suburb of St. Louis, where they joined the 200-member Kirkwood Church of Christ. It also happened that the church's minister moved away during the summer of 1968, leaving a vacancy for that position. Dan and Jeanie happened to mention that fact to my parents while visiting in Alabama. My parents told me, and I quickly applied for the job.

The Kirkwood elders invited me up for a couple of trial sermons. Sara Faye and I drove 16 hours from Abilene to St. Louis on Saturday, I preached twice on Sunday, and we drove 16 hours back to Abilene on Monday. Very soon after, the elders offered me the preaching position, which I happily accepted. Sara Faye and I still refer to our tenure from 1968-1972 in St. Louis as our "Camelot years."

After we moved to St. Louis, I learned that the Kirkwood church was unusual in one respect. As many as a third of its member families had roots in congregations for which Carl Ketcherside once preached, and they still appreciated his constructive influence in their lives. For them, his name conjured pleasant memories of past blessing, not the fearful specter of an unknown bogeyman. Unknown to me in advance, this made the Kirkwood congregation quite unique among all the churches to which I might have looked for a preaching position. It is certain that I never could have found it on my own.

Nothing is Wasted in God's Hands

Nothing entrusted to God's hand is ever wasted. Not even my six years as a typesetter in Alabama, immediately before we moved to Houston in 1982. I have already described the mounting frustration I felt about that job and how diligently I prayed to find another one.

One day early in 1981, shortly after I began searching for another job, I received a distinct inner impression that a major positive change was just over the horizon. This conception was implanted so vividly in my mind that I mentioned it to my wife. "I can't explain this," I told her, "but I have a very strong feeling that a door will open for us this next year into a future so expansive that we cannot now imagine it." That premonition, which I believe God sent to encourage me at a time of deep despondency, became reality in 1982 with the invitation to move to Houston as founding editor of *The Good Newspaper*.

The invitation came from Michael, a devout Baptist layman and professional contractor whose company built science laboratories. Michael had a vision for an interdenominational Christian newspaper, and he had begun a nationwide search for a founding editor. To further his dream, Mike formed a nonprofit corporation. He then gathered a board of directors composed of six dedicated Christian laymen across a wide denominational spectrum. There were two Baptists besides Michael—Charlie, a salesman, and Bob, an attorney. Another attorney, Tom, was active in a Methodist church. Herman was an Episcopalian and an architect. Peter, an economist for an international oil company, served as an elder in a Bible church.

After preliminary correspondence and telephone calls, Michael flew me to Houston for an interview with the board of directors. At the close of our breakfast interview, Michael said, "You go back to the print shop and we'll go about our business. Together let's all seek God's guidance. When we feel we know his will, we will be in touch."

I had been back at work for several weeks when I received another premonition one night near the close of 1981. "I cannot explain it," I said again to Sara Faye, "but I feel that Michael is going to call me within the next few days and offer me the newspaper job. If he does, are you willing to move to Houston?"

"Sure," she said. "We're in this together. I don't relish the idea of leaving my house and friends here, or moving farther away from my parents, but if you feel this is what God wants you to do, I'll support your decision."

The next morning at the print shop I had a lull between jobs and was reading Keith Miller's devotional book *Habitation of Dragons*. In that particular chapter, the author talked about trusting God by leaving the familiar and stepping into the unknown. Miller concluded the chapter with a prayer which said, in effect: "Lord, let me not be afraid today to do what seems best for me and my family; let me know today that I am free to go or to stay."

Just then the telephone rang and someone shouted across the print shop, "Fudge, it's for you—long distance!" It was Michael in Houston. "The board has just concluded a breakfast meeting," he said, and we all feel it is God's will for us to offer you the job. Do you have an impression of his leading?"

"Yes," I said, and told him about the incident the night before, and the devotional and prayer I had read minutes before.

Some time after the paper was up and running, the publisher and I were sharing stories over lunch one day of God's faithfulness in our lives, and I told him of my frustration during the six years at the print shop. Michael grinned from ear to ear. "I had about 50 applicants from all over the United States," he said, "and I narrowed the list to about a dozen finalists. Would you like to know why I selected you for this job?"

"Sure."

"Of all the applicants," he said, "you were the only person with typesetting experience. I thought that might come in handy some day."

Our Critics May Be Doing God's Work

God not only guides in unexpected ways. Sometimes he works through people who appear to be adversaries, and through circumstances that we would rather not encounter. That was certainly how God led us to the Bering Drive Church of Christ after we arrived in Houston. We had heard of that congregation before moving to Texas, and we eagerly drove 20 miles to visit it on our first Sunday in Houston. To our surprise and disappointment, we did not seem to fit in. So we decided to locate a church nearer our home. We did not know it then, but I am now quite confident that God had other work in progress, of which this temporary sidetrack was a part.

Soon we began visiting a small, new congregation close to where we lived. The people there were eager to grow in number, and they repeatedly urged us to join. That stopped, however, after someone invited me to lead worship one Sunday night and another member decided to check me out. That member contacted a local preacher friend, who telephoned a preacher he knew in Athens, Alabama. That person told him that I was "soft" on baptism, and that for several years I had been in a church that wasn't even a Church of Christ, namely the nondenominational Elm Street Church.

When the good people at the church we were visiting learned all this, they became nervous and less welcoming. I did not detect any change in the mood, but my wife did, and I promptly accused her of being cynical and unchristian. When I finally figured out what she had sensed instinctively, we instantly agreed to find another church, having enjoyed enough controversy and suspicion in our lives already to last for quite a while. So we returned to Bering Drive, and this time we felt warmly received. Soon we were assimilated into the congregation and active in its ministries.

But God was not through with this story. Five or six years later, I received a telephone call from the Houston preacher who had investigated me in Alabama. "Can we get together for lunch?" he asked. "I have some questions I would like to discuss with you." When we met, he told me that he had been restudying a particular traditional doctrine, and he shared some concerns he had on the subject. We had a delightful time together, and parted.

A few weeks later he called to request another meeting. I invited him to my home. When he arrived, he appeared uncomfortable and somewhat embarrassed. "I owe you an apology," he began. He proceeded to tell me how the suspicious brother had asked him about me years before, and how he had made inquiries of the other preacher in Alabama. I did not indicate that I knew these things already, but assured him that I was confident he had acted in good faith and with the best of intentions. I also explained how God had used that incident to lead us to Bering Drive.

"I have another question," he continued. "The most conservative elder in my congregation wants me to preach a sermon on baptism. Frankly, I am not satisfied with any of my old sermons. I wonder whether you have any insights on that topic you could share?"

I encouraged him to begin with Jesus, and to show how baptism expresses faith in the finished work of redemption Jesus accomplished on the cross for us sinners. He seemed delighted with this approach, and promised to inform me of the results of his sermon.

A few weeks later he called again, obviously very excited. "The elder who requested that I preach on baptism told me it was the best sermon he had ever heard on the subject," my friend reported. "And a man who has been attending church for many years requested to be baptized. He asked me, 'Do you wonder why I made that decision today and not before? Because all those years you tried to get me into the baptistry and I was determined that you would not succeed. But today you preached Jesus, and it made me want to be baptized.'"

God Places People and Controls Timing

My transition from religious editor to litigation attorney also resulted from divine guidance in the timely placement of specific individuals at critical steps along the way. Beginning about 1984, Houston's oil-based economy took a nosedive, and it quickly became clear that the financial base of *The Good Newspaper* was rapidly eroding with the economy. July 13, 1984 also marked my 40th birthday, which I found emotionally difficult. Topping it all, I had a recurrence of a chronic cough that lingered throughout the summer. The cough weakened me physically and depressed me emotionally.

I began looking for other job possibilities without success. Interestingly, almost ten percent of the members at Bering Drive church were attorneys. Among them was Al, who taught at one of Houston's three accredited law schools. Al also faithfully attended the Bible class I taught on Sunday mornings. "Did you ever think of going to law school?" he asked me one day. I had not, but thought it sounded interesting.

"Can someone begin law school at age 40?" I asked. He assured me that many students older than I had enrolled. I asked Sara Faye what she thought about it. Her immediate response was very practical. "I've already worked once to put you through graduate school," she said. "I don't know if I want to do it again or not." I assured her that, with God's help, this degree ought to be more financially rewarding than the first one, and she good-heartedly agreed to support me in whatever I decided to do.

I took the prerequisite LSAT and applied to two local schools. I also kept looking for another job, and asked God to open and close doors according to his will. Both law schools accepted me for admission. In January 1985, I began 40 continuous months of law school, while working fulltime as a law clerk in three successive downtown Houston firms where various Bering members were partners.

It was an ordeal, to be sure, even more strenuous than I had anticipated in advance. But, with God's help and my family's constant encouragement, I finished the course. In May of 1988, I was awarded the degree of Doctor of Jurisprudence from the University of Houston College of Law. The following month, I was licensed by the Texas Supreme Court to practice law in all the courts of that great state.

I had hoped, when I graduated from law school, to receive a job offer from the firm at which I was working at that time. That did not happen, I later learned, because two of its many partners objected to my experience as a preacher. This occurred even though my resume had described my previous Christian experience and activities in a somewhat roundabout way, highlighting aspects that I thought would interest secular employers. After this rejection, I decided to rework my resume. I did so, stating details of my religious training and experience clearly, directly and in a forthright manner. If any other potential employer might have a problem with these facts, I wanted them to encounter it immediately.

Shortly before my graduation from law school, an attorney friend from church named Rolfe kindly advised me concerning seeking a position. "At your age," he said, "none of the larger firms will probably hire you. They want to train young people in their own image, and you already have many years of adult opinions. I don't want to discourage you, but I also don't want to see you set unrealistic goals and be disappointed." His opinion was significant, since he had graduated from Harvard Law School and had helped to establish a major Houston law firm years before.

About that same time, Claudia, also an attorney at our church, invited me to submit a resume to the downtown firm of Jenkens & Gilchrist, which she had recently joined. One of the ten largest law firms in Texas, J & G, as we called it, had recently decided to enlarge its Houston office by adding 20 or 30 new attorneys. Leaving the matter entirely in God's hands, I sent in my resume, replete with religious references.

Within a week after submitting the resume, I received a telephone call from Cathy at J & G. As the person in charge of reviewing resumes and arranging interviews, she said she liked my resume very much, and she invited me to come in and meet the firm's Houston partners. I accepted her invitation, and the interviews were all positive. Shortly afterward, I received a very nice letter from the local managing partner of Jenkens & Gilchrist, offering me a position as an attorney with the firm.

Just after I came to J & G, Cathy left to pursue other interests. Before she left, however, she told me that she was a devout Catholic with a master's degree in Christian education. My obvious religious references had caught her eye, she said, as she reviewed a large stack of more normal legal resumes.

A year or two later, my experienced friend Rolfe, who had encouraged me not to expect to work for the larger firms, telephoned me at the office. "I haven't told anyone else this yet," he said, "but I am considering leaving the firm I helped to start many years ago. Jenkens & Gilchrist is a highly respected firm," he continued, "and I wonder whether they might have a place for my area of practice in the Houston office." I immediately relayed the information to our managing partner. Before long, Rolfe was on board as a partner with Jenkens & Gilchrist. For the next two years, four of us attorneys from Bering Drive Church of Christ enjoyed working together at that law firm's Houston office.

Rolfe's earlier advice to me when I was graduating from law school had been on target. It correctly reflected the ordinary state of affairs. However, the ironic wrinkle in this story reminded me once again that life under God's guidance is anything but "ordinary," and that nothing is impossible with God.

Human Calamities are God's Opportunities

Even apparent calamity is often a tool of God's guidance. That truth became clear when I was suddenly laid off from Jenkens & Gilchrist, just as our daughter Melanie was about to graduate from high school and enroll at Abilene Christian University. After three years of building a Houston presence, during the spring and summer of 1991, the law firm suddenly terminated 29 of its 39 Houston attorneys.

Dan, the local managing partner, came into my office that day with a grim look on his face. "Edward," he said kindly, "I have to tell you something, and this may be the most difficult thing I have had to do in my legal career." Then he told me the bad news.

As soon as Dan left, I bowed my head and committed the matter to the Lord. "Father," I said, "you are in charge and you are faithful. I accept whatever your will may be. You know our circumstances and needs, and I ask you to continue to provide them. Thank you that you will do that." Then, taking a yellow legal pad from my desk, I began writing the names of local attorneys and judges I knew, who also were dedicated believers. Within a few minutes, I had filled three pages with names.

At home I assembled the whole family, including Melanie and Jeremy, then ages 18 and 15. "I don't know what is going to happen," I told them, "but I know that God will take care of us somehow. Your mother and I have been through many difficulties these past 24 years, and the Lord has always been faithful. It will be exciting to see how he provides this time, and then we will all give him thanks together." We held hands and I tried to lead a prayer, but kept choking up with emotion and could not speak. Finally Melanie said, "Amen!" sending us on our way.

(A year later, during a visit home from university, Melanie thanked me for including her and Jeremy in this adventure. "I knew that God had done many wonderful things for you and Mother in years past," she said. "This situation gave me an opportunity to see for myself how God works and answers prayer, and the experience strengthened my own faith.")

Over the next week, I began calling the people I had listed on the yellow pad. I explained what had occurred, requested that they remember me in prayer, and asked them to inform me if they heard of an opening that I might be able to fill. As I neared the bottom of my list, I came upon the name of Bob Simmons. A friend for several years, Bob had been a board member of *The Good Newspaper*. He was a teacher in the nondenominational Bible Study Fellowship, and a Sunday School teacher and deacon at his Baptist church. So I called Bob and made my little speech. He was silent for a moment. "It s very interesting that you called just now," he finally said. "I've been sitting here at my desk praying for some more help."

Within ten days, God presented me with four good job opportunities, including an offer from Bob's firm. The fourth call came one day at home, as I was standing in the kitchen with Sara Faye. I answered the ringing phone, and found myself talking to Carlene, the partner of a downtown firm with whom I had interviewed earlier. She and her partner Danny had discussed my call, she said. She was inviting me for a second interview to discuss salary and other terms of employment. Suddenly I heard myself saying, "Thank you very much for the honor, but I've decided to accept a position with the firm of Simmons & Fletcher."

"When did you decide that?" Sara Faye asked in astonishment, after I finished the call. "Just this second, I suppose," I said. "I suddenly felt it was what I was supposed to do."

That abrupt conviction was confirmed almost daily during the six years following, as Bob and I shared deeply in our walks of faith. I was also enriched by fellowship with Bob's co-owner Keith Fletcher, a Presbyterian elder and Sunday School teacher, as well as with a variety of other Christian attorneys and staff personnel.

Soon after my arrival, the attorneys and non-attorney managers in our firm began to gather every month for informal, early-morning prayer meeting and Bible study. That led to a weekend management retreat, at which we produced an official purpose statement for the law firm, explicitly affirming our Christian principles and goals.

Although the firm was completely non-discriminatory in employment and advancement, attorneys and staff alike had complete freedom to witness or minister to clients or anyone else as we felt led. We also tried to make the purpose statement our daily goal, namely "to serve God" by helping our clients "in a prompt and caring manner, while modeling Christian attitudes and behavior." Through the years I was there, God gave me favor at the firm, where the letterhead eventually said: "Simmons, Fletcher & Fudge."

In 1997, through a totally unexpected series of events which someone else initiated, I suddenly left that employment to join the firm of Lanier, Parker & Sullivan in downtown Houston. This change also involved extraordinary timing of events, alignment of persons and, later, what I perceived to be a prophetic word. That story will have to wait for another time.

Exciting to Live by Faith!

Unlike many individuals who have planned out their entire lives and worked hard to accomplish those plans, I have hardly had to plan any major part of my life. Not that I have not tried, but rather that my own plans and expectations so often run counter to God's. I must admit that I have often wondered what in the world God was doing.

However, in retrospect, I see that his way has always been best. I can never "doubt his tender mercy, who through life has been my Guide." I also know better now what Homer Hailey meant, many years ago, when he told our Bible class at Florida College, "It's an exciting adventure to walk by faith!" Not always joyful. Not always free of stress. But "exciting"? No doubt about it!

TO REFLECT OR DISCUSS

1. As you reflect over your own life so far, can you see God's hand guiding you at times through "open and closed doors"?

2. Some Christians view circumstances as merely "luck" or "chance." Is that approach consistent with biblical faith?

3. Consider the stories of the destruction of Sodom, the Exodus from Egypt, and of Jonah (for starters). How might a believer and an unbeliever explain these events differently?

Chapter 13

Where from Here?

Wherever He may guide me,
*   no want shall turn me back;*
My shepherd is beside me,
*   and nothing can I lack.*
His wisdom ever waketh,
*   His sight is never dim;*
He knows the way He taketh,
*   and I will walk with Him.*

–Anna L. Waring

It should go without saying that this recital of my own encounters with the living God is neither exhaustive nor normative for anyone else. We are talking about an individual relationship with a personal God. However, the Bible assures us that God is no respecter of persons, and that he eagerly desires relationship with any person who persistently and humbly seeks his company—anyone who is willing to sacrifice whatever stands in the way.

God's Blessing is for Sinners

That commitment does not require sinless perfection, otherwise no human being who has ever lived could enjoy relationship with God, except Jesus Christ himself. Abraham was a liar.

Moses was a murderer. David was an adulterer. God does not guide us because we are good; he guides us because he is good. He blesses us, not because we are faithful, but because he is faithful. That was true of ancient Israel. It was the case with Jesus' own Apostles. It is no different today.

I find that very encouraging, since I am also a sinner who constantly falls short of God's ideal for human life. As with the truth of God's guidance, I have also learned the truth of my own sinfulness by experience. As a child, I knew that I was a sinner because the Bible says that all are sinners. As an adult, I have encountered to some extent the darkness that is in me. I have seen how near the surface it lies. I have discovered something of its persistence and insatiability. I have also been confounded and knocked to the ground by its pervasiveness. One story will make that point clear without embarrassing anyone else.

About 1982, shortly before we moved from Alabama to Texas, I was invited to participate in an independent theological seminar, held on the campus of Vanderbilt University in Nashville, Tennessee. I considered the invitation a great honor and was highly gratified to receive it. While driving up to Nashville from Alabama, a trip of about two hours, I began to thank God for the opportunity I had been given. Soon, however, gratitude subtly began to mutate into pride, as I reflected on how richly I deserved this honor; how, in fact, it had been so long time in coming.

After a period of self-congratulation, I was suddenly smitten with an attack of conscience. In an instant, my eyes were opened to the pride underlying all these musings. I remembered God's word to me a few years before about the gifts he had given me, and concerning my responsibility to use them faithfully to his glory. At that realization, I genuinely repented before God, and began to pray aloud in confession and humility.

I had barely begun that prayer when another notion filled my mind. "What a fine prayer of repentance!" I thought. "I do not think I have ever heard a more wonderful expression of humility." At that point, I knew that my own fallen nature was past remedy. I could then only say with the Apostle Paul, "O wretched man that I am!"

It serves no useful purpose to describe my sins in detail, but those who know me best can bear witness to the temptations with which I struggle daily. Even they do not know as well as I do the tenacity of my fallen nature—of the mulish recurrence of selfishness, lust and pride—and I do not see it nearly as accurately as God. Does God guide sinful people? Except for his only-begotten Son, God has never had any other people with which to work.

Our Stories and The Story

We should never confuse our own experiences with the gospel. Our stories are not the primary one. That is the story of God's faithfulness to Jesus of Nazareth, who, by his faithfulness to God, justified the Father's forgiveness of sinners and reconciled us to the God who loved us all the time. Our stories are always secondary to the Gospel story.[1] But that does not mean they are unimportant.

If the Psalms provide any indication, God is pleased when his people publicly declare his mighty acts on their behalf. The prophet Malachi envisions a time when those who know the Lord speak often to one another about their walk with the Lord and their experiences in his company. The author of the Epistle to the Hebrews, like the Psalmist whom he quotes, encourages us to report God's works to the believing community.

Let's renew that practice in churches where the fire once burned brighter than it does now! Let's create such opportunities for sincere, heart-felt witnessing in churches that have never enjoyed that practice! And, while we are at it, let's turn the topic of ordinary, daily conversations to God and his wonderful works. Heaven knows we chat about everything else—matters far less significant than this.

God is Still the Great Shepherd

In the beloved and familiar Shepherd Psalm, which most Christians can quote, David expressed his confidence concerning the future: "Surely goodness and mercy shall follow me all the days of my life, and I will dwell in the house of the LORD forever." Did you ever notice the connection between that statement and the comments just before it? How could David know this? What was the basis of his confidence?

It was just this" God had never let him down before. God had been there every step of the way—providing, leading and protecting David according to his will. Based on that demonstration of divine power and faithfulness throughout the past, David could be sure that God would shepherd him in the future. Because God is God, David could even affirm that he would have the final word over death itself. We have every reason to surpass David in this confidence. For we know about God's faithfulness in Jesus Christ, whom God raised from the dead.

For many years, I dreaded the arrival of my fiftieth birthday, because my father died at age 57. About three months before I turned 50, the Lord graciously removed that anxiety as he spoke to me again through a particular verse of Scripture. This time it was the Psalm that said, "The LORD will fulfill his purpose for me."

As I complete this revised edition of this book, I am approaching my 58th birthday. I do not know how long I will live, of course, and neither do you. But we can know, without any doubt whatsoever, that our times are in God's hands. He will fulfill his purpose for all of us who put our lives in his keeping.

In that confidence, we may say with the blind songwriter, Fanny J. Crosby, in the words of her well-known hymn:

> All the way my Savior leads me:
> What have I to ask beside?
> Can I doubt his tender mercy,
> Who thro' life has been my guide?

Heav'nly peace, divinest comfort,
Here by faith in Him to dwell!
For I know, whate'er befall me,
Jesus doeth all things well.

All the way my Savior leads me,
O the fullness of His love!
Perfect rest to me is promised
In my Father's house above.

When my spirit, clothed immortal,
Wings its flight to realms of day,
This my song, thro' endless ages,
Jesus led me all the Way!

TO REFLECT OR DISCUSS

1. Does your current church fellowship provide any opportunity for sharing God's works in your life? If not, how might you encourage or create such opportunities?

2. How does God's faithfulness to Jesus Christ inspire confidence that he will keep all his promises to us?

3. Think about the Psalmist's affirmation that "the LORD will fulfill his purpose for me." How does such an assurance shape the way you might view your own life on earth?

4. Will you think or live any differently because of reading this book? If so, in what way?